AF406388

SUSTAINABLE SPIRITUALITY

MAINTAINING FAITH IN THE FACE OF ADVERSITY

BY RICH NELSON

First Edition published August 2016
Second Edition published September 2024

A Broken Hill Publication
Glenwood Springs, Colorado

www.srnelson.com

"Peace I leave with you, my peace I give unto you: not as the world giveth, give I unto you. Let not your heart be troubled, neither let it be afraid."

John 14:27 (KJV)

Contents

This book is lovingly dedicated to my beautiful wife, Connie, who provided the idea for the book and, through her Christ-like example, the inspiration for me to write it.

PREFACE

The fundamental principle of Christianity is faith in the Lord Jesus Christ. We accept Him as our Lord and Savior and look forward to when He returns to reign as King of kings. The Second Coming of Christ is mentioned over 1,500 times in the Old Testament and over 300 times in the New Testament. It has often been prophesied that the Second Coming will be a time of pessimism, fear, discouragement, and despair.

Luke describes the prevailing conditions in the last days as a time of "signs in the sun and the moon and the stars, and on the earth nations will be in distress, anxious over the roaring of the sea and the surging waves.

People will be fainting from fear and the expectation of what is coming in the world, for the powers of the heavens will be shaken."[1]

Today, we cautiously watch as humanity's structures begin to crumble. Global alliances are strained as political turmoil runs rampant. The war on terror does little to stop terrorism yet continues to cost precious lives. From commerce to health care, from fiscal policies to food production, our society is falling apart.

Marriage is assailed and attacked, and more than half end in divorce. Children are viewing pornography, taking drugs and alcohol, and becoming pregnant before graduating high school.

The world's privileged few buy summer homes in the south of France while nearly a billion others around the world face starvation. We question the morality of how some people "own pennies in a jar" while others "own oil tankers." We deliberate over

---

[1] Luke 21:25,26 (NET).

why "some spend winter in a palace; some spend it in blankets." [2]

And so we send out bell ringers at Christmas time and set up yard sales to raise money to feed the poor, clean the air, save the latest endangered species, or whatever the most recent popular cause is. We develop programs to provide birth control in high school and set up student daycare services. We offer no-fault, low-cost divorce so that everyone can participate. We mount massive drug awareness education programs and expand our drug rehabilitation centers, all the while fighting to legalize recreational drug use. We are applying a Band-Aid® to a gaping, open wound while slashing our wrists all at the same time.

These are not sustainable solutions to society's dilemmas. They address symptoms of the disease, not the disease itself. We are merely hacking away at the weeds, leaving the roots of sin firmly in place beneath the soil.

---

[2] From *Get Up Off Our Knees*, by The Housematins, London 0 Hull 4, 1986.

Paul warned us that "in the last days difficult times will come. For people will be lovers of themselves, lovers of money, boastful, arrogant, blasphemers, disobedient to parents, ungrateful, unholy, unloving, irreconcilable, slanderers, without self-control, savage, opposed to what is good, treacherous, reckless, conceited, loving pleasure rather than loving God. They will maintain the outward appearance of religion but will have repudiated its power." [3] Well, that pretty much sums up our day and times!

But there is a solution. It requires a return to the Spirit of Truth. It requires replacing Jesus Christ and his teachings in our society, government, schools, and, most significantly, in our own hearts and minds.

Why is it necessary to center our confidence, hope, and trust in the one solitary figure of Jesus of Nazareth? Why is faith in him essential for peace of mind in this life and hope in the world to come? And how do we avoid

---

[3] 2 Timothy 3: 1-5 (NET).

getting caught up in the prevailing pessimism and fatalism of the last days?

Our answers to these questions will determine whether we face the future with a sustainable spirituality that gives us courage, hope, and optimism or whether we fall into apprehension, anxiety, and despair like the rest of the world.

I know many do not believe in God and regard religion as nothing more than fantasy and fallacy. They are convinced that humanity can, on its own, surmount the world's troubles and fix society's problems through its own resourcefulness and ingenuity. But they are building their houses on sand. God cannot continue to withhold the prophesied cataclysm that comes from sin.

In turbulent and troubling times, the Christian pathway can seem almost too challenging to travel. How do we maintain our feet on the footholds of faith as the prophesied future unfolds? If we regard Christianity as nothing more than a bundle of beliefs and behaviors we painstakingly carry on our shoulders, it could appear overwhelming.

But for the disciples of Christ who are spiritually prepared to sustain their belief and maintain their faith, their devotion becomes not a burden but a blessing. Christianity is not a weight on their shoulders but, rather, wings on their backs. It brings light in dark times and sweetens the bitter cup of adversity. It sustains them in the flaming furnace of fear and comforts them in the deep pits of despair. Christianity is the assurance of a qualified Captain on the very rough voyage of life.

The Christian pathway is the comforting assurance of an everlasting light that shines in the darkest night and an eternal warmth felt within the loneliest heart. This is the power of that sustainable hope, which is provided as a gift to all of us through the pure love of Christ.

This book's purpose is to help us look carefully and honestly into our own lives to prevent the development of any spiritual infirmity that could destroy our faith, particularly in light of the warnings about the last days. It is a call to prepare ourselves for the day when all of society's houses built on sand will tumble around us.

But as we reposition our lives to be closer to God, he will become closer to us, and we will develop even greater spiritual sustainability through increased faith in Christ. Sustainable spirituality intensifies as we follow Christ's teachings.

Jesus taught: "I am the way, and the truth, and the life. No one comes to the Father except through me." [4]

He did not just bring light into a darkened and fallen world; Jesus is the light.

He embodies hope, illuminating our paths with truth and love and guiding us through life's trials and tribulations. his presence dispels fear and doubt, revealing the way to peace and salvation.

As the Light of the World, Jesus invites us to reflect that light in our own lives. We are called to be beacons of hope for others, sharing compassion and kindness in a society often overshadowed by despair. In each act of love, we carry forward his message—that even in

---

[4] John 14:6.

moments of deepest darkness, there is always a source of radiant hope.

His teachings encourage us to seek understanding over judgment and mercy over condemnation. Through his example, He showed us how to shine brightly amidst adversity—embracing those who are marginalized or suffering while firmly standing against injustice.

He didn't just teach the truth; Jesus is the truth.

His life embodied the principles he preached—compassion, love, forgiveness, and humility. Through his parables and actions, he illuminated a path for humanity to follow that transcends time and culture.

He revealed profound insights into human nature and divine purpose in every interaction. He challenged societal norms and offered solace to the brokenhearted. He provided physical healing and addressed deeper spiritual needs with each miracle performed.

His message of unconditional love called on people to embrace their neighbors as themselves, breaking barriers of race, class, and belief. In a world often filled with division and strife, Jesus stood as a unifying figure who invited all to partake in God's grace.

He did not merely make the resurrection available; Jesus is the resurrection and the life.

This profound truth emphasizes that through Him, we gain access to eternal life—a life that transcends mere existence and offers a deep, abiding relationship with God. In moments of despair or grief, when death seems final, and hope feels distant, it is in Christ that we find assurance and comfort. He embodies victory over death, demonstrating that physical demise does not have the last word.

Jesus' declaration invites us to trust Him as more than a historical figure; He is our source of strength and renewal. Through his teachings, actions, and sacrificial love, He reveals the nature of true life—one characterized by peace, joy, purpose, and powerful transformation. In knowing Jesus as the resurrection and the life, believers are encouraged to live boldly amidst trials because their future is secure in Him.

As we walk through life, we are reminded that each moment carries significance within God's plan. The promise of resurrection ignites our faith—it empowers us to share this good news with others who search for meaning beyond their circumstances. Embracing Jesus as both the resurrection and the life shapes how we connect within ourselves and with those around us; it compels us to be agents of love while offering hope amid hopelessness.

The most significant benefit and blessing to this world would be for men and women everywhere to practice the pure love of Christ. Christ's pure love is simple kindness. It is humility and patience. It is a selfless love that asks for nothing in return. It does not tolerate evil or delight in sin. It condemns ridicule, vulgarity, and abuse. A heart filled with Christ's love has no place for bigotry, hatred, or violence. It encourages diverse people to live together in Christian love regardless of religious belief, race, nationality, financial standing, education, or culture.

The pure love of Christ will fortify us and help us sustain our faith and spirituality even through the most challenging tribulations and turmoil. Our hope for peace and happiness in this world and eternal glory hereafter are intrinsically tied to our Lord and Savior, Jesus Christ, the Hope of Israel.

CHAPTER ONE

THE FORGOTTEN SIDE OF SUSTAINABILITY

Sustainable is one of the popular terms tossed about in today's social salad to educate us on creating a more conscientious way of living. Sustainability relates to a strategy taken by the present population aimed at not diminishing the expectations of future populations to enjoy similar levels of consumption, wealth, utility, or welfare.

In environmental science, sustainability is the capability to survive and endure; it is how biological systems continually remain diverse and productive. One definition of sustainable is to keep in existence, to maintain. I like this definition. It is concise and to the point. As a rule, sustainability is simply the endurance of systems and processes.

Sustainable living has become a social challenge that has taken on many forms. Restructured living conditions have created ecovillages and sustainable cities. Adjustments in trade and industry have given us sustainable agriculture and architecture. Science continues to develop "greener" technologies and more renewable energy sources. People worldwide are constantly making lifestyle changes to conserve our natural resources.

The global attention given to sustainability primarily focuses on the physical environment, which is currently facing urgent issues of environmental degradation, climate change, overconsumption, population growth, and society's pursuit of open-ended economic development in a closed system. These challenges will not be easily mended under the current practices of materialistic self-indulgence, science-based skepticism, and political radicalism. We all must take action to address these issues.

Despite the increased popularity of the term "sustainability," the likelihood that human societies will attain environmental sustainability remains in question. Very little attention, however, is given to the spiritual aspects of sustainability, without which the world floats rudderless on an angry sea of cataclysmic disasters and exceptional challenges that threaten to overwhelm us daily.

Throughout the world, humanity experiences growing anxiety and fear. For some, these fears and worries may seem increasingly close at hand, but these heart-troubling emotions are already a constant, persistent, and foreboding presence for many others. This constraining fear does not come from the hazards of our circumstances but from the failure of the human heart as it becomes separated from its spiritual nature.

Natural disasters have occurred with increasing regularity in recent years. Devastating earthquakes have leveled cities in numerous parts of the world; great storms and hurricanes have ravaged towns and shorelines; damaging and deadly floods have washed through Europe, Asia, and the Americas.

Major storms seriously affect transportation and food supplies. We continually see reports of long lines at grocery stores as victims of natural disasters try to purchase food supplies and drinkable water.

Other signs of the times include political, social, and economic events that likewise test our spiritual sustainability in distinct ways. Economic instability is commonplace today. We witness disheartening recessions, extensive unemployment, demoralizing depressions, and skyrocketing inflation, which can be as disastrous as a major earthquake. War and widespread terrorism are becoming the norm in many countries.

It doesn't always take a natural or man-made disaster to test a person's spiritual stability. Even routine daily living can seriously test our physical, mental, emotional, and spiritual health parameters. The prophet Moses wrote in his time of the "terror within" and the "sword without" destroying a nation not grounded on a spiritual foundation. In these challenging times, it's important to remember that spiritual stability can provide us peace and comfort. [5]

The shepherds "were absolutely terrified" when the angel appeared to announce Jesus' birth. So much so that the angel consoled them with the words, "Do not be afraid." [6] Jesus ended his earthly ministry telling his apostles: "Peace I leave with you; my peace I give to you; I do not give it to you as the world does. Do not let your hearts be distressed or lacking in courage." [7]

How can we, as faithful Christians, remain perfectly calm and serene among all the convulsions of the earth—the turmoil, strife, war, pestilence, famine, and distress of nations? How do we "keep in existence" our faith? How do we "maintain" our level of spirituality, sustain our peace, and not allow our hearts to "be distressed or lacking in courage?"

We knew beforehand that such things would transpire on earth. We understand the meaning behind these events and view them in their true light. In the Bible, God tells us what

---

[5] Deuteronomy 32:25, 28-29 (NET).
[6] Luke 2:9-10 (NET).
[7] John 14:27 (NET).

will happen so that we can prepare for and live through these upsetting times without losing faith. The most significant portion of our personal preparation rests through our knowledge and understanding of Biblical prophecies.

Three critical areas of personal preparation will assist believing Christians in facing the distress of troubling times with faith, courage, and hope:

1.   Knowledge and understanding of world events,

2.   physical provision and readiness, and

3.   spiritual preparation.

We should each be responsible for our own mental, physical (including economic), and spiritual sustainability.

A Knowledge of World Events

The judgments that precede Christ's coming will profoundly affect the world's nations. Significant changes are taking place around the world. For those watching (not with physical eyes but with eyes of faith), things that make newspaper headlines or the evening news are seen as partial fulfillment, at least, of events prophesied centuries ago. The only way we can recognize the hand of God in all these happenings is to keep informed of world events and know what is happening around us.

Jesus declared to his disciples over two millennia ago that "this gospel of the kingdom will be preached throughout the whole inhabited earth as a testimony to all the nations, and then the end will come." [8] With the advent of radio, television, the internet, and social media, we have seen this prophecy fulfilled in our lifetime. As certainly as this prophecy has been fulfilled, God's purposes will continue to unfold in our view if we have eyes that see and minds that know and understand.

One pivotal step to preparing for the Second Coming is gaining more knowledge and understanding. Some of that knowledge will come to us as we read and study God's word. But we must also be educated and knowledgeable about the world around us and the rising events that are part of his magnificent

----

[8] Matthew 24:14 (NET).

plan leading up to the return of his Son to reign as King of kings.

Physical Provision and Readiness

We need to develop our personal sustainability practices in five distinct areas. They are:

1. Education,
2. Employment,
3. Health,
4. Survival Preparedness, and
5. Financial Management.

Before God's final judgments transpire, our personal sustainability could be extensively strained and tested. If we have adequately prepared ourselves, our hearts need not be distressed or lacking in courage. We can then reliably receive the peace that Christ offers us.

Physical provision and readiness will be vital to our personal sustainability in the turbulent times to come. We could quickly become isolated from customary transportation methods, business, and community connections. Recent natural disasters have demonstrated that infrastructures supporting our day-to-day living are incredibly fragile and complex.

With even a minor earthquake, freeway overpasses could collapse, disrupting traffic flow in and out of a city. Food and other needed commodities would be unable to reach the marketplaces. A single incident can put an entire city into crisis without warning. The growing threat of local terrorism can bring widespread social disruption and could restrict a whole population from the usual avenues of provision and protection.

We have become cripplingly dependent on our current social structure for the normal functioning of our lives but may soon find ourselves separated from the usual pattern of society, which provides so many of our daily needs.

Spiritual Preparation

Spiritual preparation in a crisis is the most essential and critical aspect of our sustainability. We need not be troubled when we live in economic, political, and spiritual instability—unmistakable indications that Christ's coming is imminent.

"Peace I leave with you…. Do not let your hearts be distressed or lacking in courage." [9]

Regrettably, in many cases, our spiritual sustainability is the most neglected aspect of our preparation.

During a recent drought in the western United States, when hardly any snow or rain fell throughout December, local news stations reported the possibility of severe water shortages if circumstances did not improve. The reaction in Colorado and its surrounding states was noteworthy. One news report indicated that wheat shipments out of Idaho jumped from one truckload per week to an astonishing three truckloads daily! The purchase of food storage supplies increased 800 percent that month. Many secured property loans and mortgages to pay for emergency food supplies.

People took the threat to their physical provision and readiness very seriously, but at

---

[9] John 14:27 (NET).

the same time, was there a concurrent rise in concern over spiritual sustainability? Was there an 800 percent increase in prayer during that same time? Did Bible reading increase significantly that month? Was there a considerable increase in church attendance?

We hurried to stock up on our physical supplies. Did we also hurriedly turn to our God with an increased desire to strengthen and fortify our spiritual sustainability?

We do not know when the calamities and troubles of the last days will fall upon us. The Lord has withheld from us the day and hour of his coming. He tells us to watch and be ready. As Christians, we must prepare, watch, and wait. There are no guarantees in this life except the guarantee of accepting Christ and living righteously.

We can increase our spiritual sustainability and better prepare for the second coming by gaining more knowledge and understanding of world events, becoming self-reliant in physical provisions and readiness, and increasing our spirituality. As we continually strive to improve our spiritual sustainability, we will gain an increased perception of the Lord's promise: "Peace I leave with you; my peace I give to you; I do not give it to you as the world does. Do not let your hearts be distressed or lacking in courage." [10]

If we experience any anxiety over the day of vengeance when the Lord will return, we should let our anxiety be centered on the sanctification of our hearts, the purifying of our desires, and on preparing for the events that are rushing toward us. We must seek the Spirit of Christ to prepare for the days ahead.

---

[10] John 14:27 (NET).

CHAPTER TWO

SUSTAINABLE SPIRITUALITY GOALS

Sustainable Development Goals (SDGs) are recommended objectives and crucial milestones for future global development. They have replaced the Millennium Development Goals (MDGs), which concluded at the end of 2015. Established in 2000, the MDGs were a significant step forward, adopted by 189 United Nations member states and over 20 international organizations.

These goals were created to advance the following sustainable development criteria by 2015:

1.   To eradicate extreme poverty and hunger.

2.   To achieve universal primary education.

3.   To promote gender equality and empower women.

4.   To reduce child mortality.

5.   To improve maternal health.

6.   To combat HIV/AIDS, malaria, and other diseases.

7.   To ensure environmental sustainability.

8.   To develop a global partnership for development.

According to data submitted to the United Nations, Cuba was the only nation in the world that met the definition of sustainable development in 2006.

Like sustainable development, achieving sustainable spirituality does not happen automatically. Sustainable spirituality is the ongoing, conscious effort to understand and carry out God's will in our lives. We need to have spiritual goals that advance us along this path. These goals should be specific, measurable, and aligned with our core values.

They can encompass various aspects of our spiritual journey, such as deepening our understanding of sacred texts, enhancing our meditation practices, or cultivating a sense of community through shared rituals and fellowship.

In setting these spiritual goals, we must regularly reflect on our progress and remain open to adjusting them as we grow. This flexibility allows us to respond to new insights or challenges that may arise along the way. Regular self-assessment helps ensure that we stay connected with the intentions behind our goals. Are they still resonating with who we are becoming? Are we allowing ourselves the grace to experience setbacks without judgment?

We might also consider incorporating service into our spiritual objectives. Acts of kindness and compassion towards others can often lead us closer to inner peace and fulfillment while reinforcing a sense of interconnectedness within the broader human experience.

By establishing clear spiritual goals and committing ourselves wholeheartedly to them, we create a roadmap for personal growth that fosters not only individual enlightenment but also positively contributes to those around us. In this pursuit lies both challenge and reward—an ongoing adventure that invites us deeper into understanding ourselves and the greater tapestry of life surrounding us.

The path of spiritual development is, for the most part, a challenging, uphill effort. We may momentarily experience a burst of faith and then encounter a personal setback somewhere along the way. Doubts arise that could leave us spiritually debilitated.

The demands and responsibilities of our jobs consume our time and distract us from spiritual matters. We become separated from the saving doctrines of Jesus. We allow "little" sins to stunt our spiritual development. It is a continuous struggle to grasp ideals that seldom remain clear and in constant focus, but God will bless our efforts to develop sustainable spiritual goals.

Spirituality doesn't just happen to us. It doesn't simply appear as we get older or more mature. Our good wishes or even excellent church attendance won't, by themselves, create it for us. More is required of us. The development of sustainable spirituality is a personal, intentional effort to understand and carry out the will of God in our lives.

Our willingness to try to set our spiritual development goals is an essential step toward spiritual sustainability. This is a proactive process. It requires desiring and planning with consistency and integrity. It requires escaping from our culturally acquired custom of spending our time and energy on pursuits that provide instantaneous and glamorous worldly rewards. The driving force behind material motivation is immediate gratification, and consequently, spiritual values take a back seat to profits and pleasures.

These cultural habits are dangerous adversaries to sustainable spirituality. Spiritual ideals always contradict the purpose and practicality of our pressing worldly values and pursuits. Meaningful truth, whether spiritual or secular, rarely reveals its cherished mysteries to the impatient or impulsive inquircr.

So, how do we nurture sustainable spirituality when the world's influences conspire to confuse, divert, and distract us? The answer lies in our ability to build a sustainable spiritual lifestyle founded on solid rock, not sand.

Sometimes, we may need to be more effective in furthering our spiritual development. But today's trials prepare us for tomorrow's triumphs. Think about that for a minute. Preparation is a present-day pursuit.

So often, we imagine that preparation relates more to the intense tests we will undergo someday. Through years of education, we prepare for the challenge of finding and keeping a job. We even take classes to prepare for childbirth. We purchase emergency supply kits in the event of some future calamity—a flood, an earthquake, a terrorist attack, or the loss of employment. We pray and study the Bible to strengthen our faith in Jesus as a means to prepare for the difficulties and distresses of the prophesied future, a time when our faith may be all we have left to rely on.

Spiritual preparation is not just a concept but a crucial aspect of our spiritual journey. It's more than simply getting ready for the future. It involves consciously aligning our thoughts, emotions, and actions with our innermost beliefs and values. This preparation can take many forms—meditation, prayer, reflection, or even community service—all of which ground us in our purpose.

To effectively prepare spiritually, one must first cultivate self-awareness. Understanding one's strengths and weaknesses allows for meaningful growth; it opens the door to an authentic engagement with divine presence or universal consciousness. Journaling practices can be particularly beneficial during this phase, providing a reflective space for individuals to articulate their thoughts and feelings.

Spiritual preparation often entails setting intentions that guide daily choices and interactions. It moves beyond wishful thinking into actionable steps driven by more profound ethos. Intention-setting helps clarify what we aspire towards on both personal and collective levels—fostering compassion in relationships or seeking clarity amidst chaos.

The journey of spiritual preparation also invites moments of surrender—a recognition that not everything is within our control. Embracing vulnerability enables us to experience profound transformation; by letting go of rigid expectations or fears about the future, we make room for growth.

Moreover, connecting with like-minded communities enriches this process. Engaging in discussions about faith traditions or exploring different philosophies exposes us to diverse perspectives while reinforcing our beliefs. These communal experiences can be powerful catalysts for growth as they foster accountability and shared wisdom.

In essence, spiritual preparation acts as the groundwork for building resilience against life's challenges. By dedicating time and energy to nurture our inner selves intentionally—and recognizing it as an ongoing practice—we empower ourselves not only personally but collectively transcend limitations along the path toward fulfillment and enlightenment.

The severe hardships ahead may or may not materialize during our lifetime. Of course, we hope they won't, no matter how much preparation we have undertaken. However, a life focused solely on the future disregards and undermines the blessings of the present that make life and living worthwhile today. Spiritual preparation is more about who we become in the present as we plan and prepare for the future.

Jesus perceptively explained the exquisite promise of preparation to his apostles the night he was to be crucified: "Don't let your heart be troubled. You believe in God. Believe also in me. In my Father's house are many mansions. If it weren't so, I would have told you. I am going to prepare a place for you. If I go and prepare a place for you, I will come again, and will receive you to myself; that where I am, you may be there also. Where I go, you know, and you know the way." [11]

Jesus has patiently and continually prepared for our spiritual development and growth. He has gone before us, and even now, he has a place prepared for us in the mansions of his Father. Jesus reaffirms for us that we "know the way." He has incredible conviction and certainty in our spiritual sustainability! If our faith in ourselves is ever lacking or diminished, surely we can lean on his faith in us for the time being.

____

[11] John 14:1-4 (WEB).

Paul tells us that we should fit our feet with the preparation that comes from the good news of peace.[12] The gospel of Christ engenders peace. Even when it is challenging to follow, stretches us to our limits, and makes us work harder than we would like, it still creates peace. With peace in our hearts, we are better prepared for anything.

In this life, we think only one thought at a time. Each thought is a choice. According to author Steven Claysen, we think about 50,000 thoughts a day. [13] With this many thoughts running through our heads each day, we certainly have some serious choices.

Each day, thousands of good choices are presented to us. We could clean out the garage or spend the time studying for a college exam. We might do some much-needed yard work or forego all that and go to lunch with a friend. These are all good, positive choices. But in the final analysis, we must still make the choice. We live only in the present moment, not in the past or the future.

---

[12] See Ephesians 6:15.
[13] Claysen, Steven, *The Power of Attraction*, Green Stem Media, 2015, pp. 72.

My wife recently experienced a situation that exemplifies the approach we should take in our spiritual preparation. She sustained an injury to her shoulder that required physical therapy. Her PT instructed her to perform an exercise called spider-walking. She was directed to "walk" her fingers up a wall three times a day. Her goal was to eventually be able to raise her hand higher than her head.

She had the faith and the determination that she would soon be able to lift her arm above her head. She spider-walked up the wall, marking her progress and achievement each day. At first, she could barely lift her arm as she stretched and extended her fingers as high as possible. Sometimes, her progress was no more than an eighth of an inch. But she celebrated each improvement. It took several months of exercising before she could finally lift her arm over her head. Two years later, she can lift, turn, and move her arm in any direction without even thinking about it.

However, she wasn't prepared to raise her arm to its normal height on her first attempt. Raising her arm over her head was simply beyond her capabilities. But she prepared to do a little better each morning than the night before. Little by little, a spider step at a time, she climbed the wall and met her ultimate goal.

Spiritual preparation can happen in small steps, too. Little by little, as we add to our spiritual sustainability in the present, we also develop spiritual strength for our future. As we increase our spiritual sustainability, it will no longer matter if our future holds raging storms or sunlit paths; we will be prepared and need not fear.

We will find within ourselves a reservoir of strength and resilience that anchors us, guiding us through both the tempests and tranquil moments of life. Each challenge we face will be met with an unwavering spirit, each joy celebrated with gratitude that stems from deep understanding.

In cultivating our spiritual sustainability, we learn to embrace impermanence; change becomes not something to dread but a natural flow of existence. We appreciate the lessons hidden in trials and recognize the beauty in every fleeting moment. Our connections with others deepen as we share this journey towards enlightenment, fostering compassion that extends beyond ourselves.

As our inner landscape flourishes, we positively impact those around us. We inspire others to embark on their own paths of growth—our transformed energy rippling outward like rings on water stirred by a single pebble thrown into stillness. Together, we create a community bound not by fear or scarcity but by hope and abundance.

Spiritual sustainability carries a profound wisdom: true peace lies not in external circumstances but within our hearts. As seasons may shift and uncertainties arise, let us remain steadfast—a luminous beacon amidst the chaos—and guide one another toward realms filled with promise and possibility. Fortified against whatever challenges await us, we step boldly into the future as co-creators of light.

So, just what should our sustainable spirituality goals consist of? The beauty of the gospel of Jesus Christ is its simplicity. Because of its simplicity, we often look past the mark and attempt to make things more complicated than they need to be. The following are a few simple goals and guidelines that will assist you in developing your spiritual strength and sustainability.

1. *Fortify your family.* Shelter your children from the onslaught of conceit, selfishness, and vanity. Secure your home against the assault of obscene and lewd cries of the world.

2. *Cultivate divine characteristics.* When we have come to "the rich knowledge of God and of Jesus our Lord" and have been given all things "necessary for life and godliness," Peter asks us to realize the potential of our divine nature by giving all diligence to the development of faith, excellence, knowledge, self-control, perseverance, godliness, brotherly kindness, and unselfish love. If you do this, your understanding of Christ will be complete and fruitful, and you will not be "nearsighted," and you "will never stumble into sin." [14] Remember that who we are is far more important than what may happen to us.

---

[14] See 2 Peter 1:2-10.

3. *Focus on Christ.* Allow your true eternal purpose to guide and direct your important life decisions. Don't become diverted by the storms and gales you encounter on life's voyage; remember why you are here and whom you serve.

4. *Put God first.* Sometimes, you may have to make choices not based on good and evil (which is easy) but on good and a little bit better good (which is much harder). Your safest and most secure choices will be made when you seek first the kingdom of God and its righteousness. [15]

5. *Build an earthly existence on rock, not on sand.* Wealth and material goods alone will never be able to protect you from peril and uncertainty, nor will they provide lasting pleasure. However, neglecting the material necessities of life could subject you to any change in the fickle winds of fortune and lessen your potential to pursue worthy goals.

Your capacity to effectively influence and regulate the stresses of daily living is significantly affected by how you handle your

---

[15] See Matthew 6:33.

physical self, circumstances, and situations. Appropriately care for and respect your physical body as a designated temple for the Holy Spirit. [16] Improve your education and communication skills and develop specific work habits that will allow you to navigate an ever-changing economy successfully.

Excellent physical health, suitable education, sensible money management, adequate emergency supplies, and smart living are essential to a safe and secure life. They will also protect you against an unforeseen future's inevitable instabilities and variables. A wise nation prepares for war in peacetime, and a wise person prepares for disaster in times of prosperity.

6. *Don't judge others.* Judging people and their situations does not rest on your shoulders. Jesus tells us, "Do not judge so that you will not be judged." [17] He took it a step further when he counseled us to fix our faults and defects before we attempt to correct and criticize others: "First remove the beam from

---

¹⁶ See 1 Corinthians 3:16.
¹⁷ Matthew 7:1 (NET).

your own eye, and then you will see clearly to remove the speck from your brother's eye." [18]

7. *Forgive.* When you forgive others and let go of grudges, criticisms, and hurt feelings, you reduce the stress, irritation, and aggravation that deprive you of peace. Remember, you are most like Jesus Christ when you forgive the wrongs of another person.

8. *Be proactive and positive.* Do whatever you can, whatever it takes, to build your spiritual sustainability, and then, in full faith, confidence, and assurance, expect to see God's salvation and his hand directing your life.

Personal and Individual Spirituality

Besides being gradual and incremental, a single step at a time, sustainable spiritual strength is personal. It's individual. What strengthens and develops your spirituality may not be the same as what strengthens and develops mine or anyone else's, for that matter.

Spirituality is not part of the church we go to or the Bible study group we read with. A

---

[18] Matthew 7:5 (NET).

church can provide increased opportunities for us to improve our understanding, increase our faith, and strengthen our spirituality, but no church can make us more spiritually sustainable if we don't act on the opportunities that God provides for us.

There are many "Thou shalt" and "Thou shalt nots" in Christianity. We are constantly instructed in what we "should" be doing and how we "ought" to be living.

You should read the Bible every day.

You ought to go to church every Sunday.

You need to pray every morning when you wake up and every night before you go to bed.

You should contribute to your church's relief fund, mission fund, or whatever other fund it has established.

Do any of those "shoulds" sound familiar to you? If so, you are not alone. But I have another "should" for you.

You should do what works best for you.

Sometimes, we have to ask ourselves what is best for us. What do we need or want at this moment? Our spiritual growth and progression are better developed when we are moved in directions that coincide with the path our hearts and minds are following at the time. When we recognize an unsatisfied need within ourselves and work to satisfy that need in honorable activity, we enhance our possibility for spiritual improvement.

So maybe you need the discipline of reading the Bible every day for an hour or so. Or you could benefit more from close social interaction with other Christians. Or your spiritual growth could be better served by witnessing to non-believers. The point is that consulting your needs and wants and acting on those desires will increase your spiritual development more than following others' expectations of what you need.

So, instead of listening to all the "shoulds" and "oughts" that assail our ears, perhaps we could make more meaningful mental statements to understand our needs better.

Rather than thinking, "I ought to go to church today," ask yourself, "How could regular, frequent church attendance add to my personal spiritual sustainability?"

As an alternative to "I should participate in the church's relief efforts," ask, "What kind of service would I enjoy doing?"

Instead of thinking, "I need to read the Bible more," ask yourself, "What has brought me the greatest joy from my scripture studies, and is there a way to improve that practice?"

Instead of telling yourself you had better say a prayer tonight, consider asking yourself, "What kind of personal communication do I have with God? How can I improve my communication skills so that my sincere prayers will be heard and answered and I will feel the influence of his Holy Spirit?"

Do you ever wonder if the Holy Spirit is interested in what's going on in your meager, little life? Do you feel that the Holy Spirit cares and is involved when you're walking to the bus stop or having lunch with a co-worker when you're tending to your children or cleaning out the basement? Sometimes, we may feel that the

Holy Spirit only shows up for church services and then sneaks off to a distant, hidden corner of the universe for the rest of the week. That is simply not true.

For most of our lives, we live outside of the church, in a daily Monday through Saturday grind. But the Holy Spirit is always promised to us. If we're not feeling the influence of the Holy Spirit more often, maybe it is because we're the ones who walk out of the church with a "See you next Sunday!" attitude.

Remember that spiritual development is individual. Find what works best for you as you build sustainable spiritual strength. God doesn't have just one mansion but "many mansions," and he doesn't expect us to acquire spiritual sustainability and strength in the same ways. Find what works best for you, and then develop those gifts.

Being a good Christian is a full-time job all by itself. We make attempts. Sometimes we succeed, but sometimes we fail. We let ourselves down, and we let the Lord down. But we improve. We progress. We act a little kinder towards others. We judge a little less, and we forgive a little more often. We don't need to harangue ourselves for not living up to every Christian responsibility. Just as with spider-walking up a wall, progression and improvement within us by a mere eighth of an inch is still progression and improvement.

Even though we tend to think in absolutes, life is not always black and white. Our time on earth is better defined as a continuum. We can look at our accomplishments and focus on the areas where we improve. We can then let go of the missed service we could have done for an elderly neighbor or the forgotten prayer for a sick friend that was left unsaid.

We can't do it all. We can honor God by giving what time we have and utilizing what strength he has given us from whatever position of spiritual sustainability we find ourselves at the moment. Jesus will take whatever we have to offer, no matter how little or insignificant, and he will make up the difference. That is the grace of God.

Every day, we can develop our spiritual sustainability in little ways. Every morning, we can reach an eighth of an inch higher than we did the night before. Listen to the needs of your own heart and spirit, and then nourish them with what they most need to grow, strengthen, and develop. Most of all, remember that you do not need to be troubled in your heart. Jesus has prepared the way and assures us that we will know the way as we walk it.

Two Dutch sisters, Betsie and Corrie Ten Boom, were imprisoned in Ravensbruck during World War II for sheltering Jews in their home. After their liberation, Corrie wrote this poignant vignette:

"Whenever large numbers of our Dutch women were sent away on transports, they were replaced by Polish women. These women had suffered a great deal and looked worn and anxious. We could not understand each other's language. Yet we suffered the same affliction side by side. The same Saviour had borne their griefs also.

"It was evening. A little woman was leaning wearily against the edge of her bed. She looked deeply unhappy. Betsie went to her, took her hand in her own, and said questioningly, "Jesoes Christoes?"

"A glow of happiness came over the face of the little woman. She drew Betsie to her and kissed her. The Name that is above every name united not only heaven and earth, but also the hearts of people of different tongues. These Polish Catholic women had such great love for their Saviour that the sound of his spoken name made their faces shine.

"We sometimes sang, 'Come to the Saviour, make no delay,' and they would sing it with us. The melody of that song had been imported from Poland by the Salvation Army. What the words were in Polish, I did not know. Someday we shall sing that song before the throne of God, and there will be no difference of language to separate us." [19]

One writer stated, "He is waiting for us to come to the mansion that he has prepared for us. He is the great measure of reality, against which other measures crumble. When his light burns in our hearts, no darkness can smother it. When he is beside us, no enemy can threaten us." [20]

---

[19] Corrie Ten Boom, *A Prisoner and Yet* . . . New York: Jove Publications, 1977, pp. 131-32.
[20] Author and source unknown.

Our spiritual strength and sustainability are in Jesus. He provides us with an unshakeable foundation, guiding us through life's challenges and uncertainties. His teachings illuminate our path, and we find hope and purpose in Him. By nurturing our relationship with Christ through prayer, worship, and community fellowship, we cultivate resilience to face adversities with grace.

Jesus exemplifies love and compassion; by following his example, we grow spiritually and contribute positively to the lives of those around us. The fruits of the Spirit—love, joy, peace—are manifestations of this connection that empower us to make a difference in the world.

As we lean on his promises and trust in his plan for our lives, we become vessels of light in dark times. Our faith enables us to rise above difficulties, knowing that God works all things for good for those who love Him. [21] Thus, anchored in Christ's unwavering support

---

[21] Romans 8:28.

and guidance, we can confidently navigate life's storms.

We may never see the severe hardships in our lives that will test and strain our faith. But every day, we can rejoice in today's blessings, prepare for tomorrow's uncertainties, and develop our spiritual sustainability and faith in the Lord and Savior who died for us, who lives in us, and who also lives in anticipation of meeting us in the mansions he has prepared for us in the Kingdom of his Father. This empowers us and encourages us to maintain our faith and spiritual strength.

CHAPTER THREE

ACHIEVING WORLD PEACE

World peace, or the concept of freedom, peace, and happiness within and between all nations and people, embraces the ideal of worldwide nonviolence through a system of restraint that would prevent warfare. It refers to ending all aggression and hostility between all humanity.

Since 1945, the United Nations, with its five permanent members of the Security Council (the UK, China, Russia, France, and the US), has been steadfast in its mission to resolve conflicts without nations resorting to war. Despite the challenges, these efforts give us hope for a future where peace prevails.

Several years ago, on the campus of a large university, a group of students demonstrated by waving large signs that read, "We demand peace." We live in troubled times. The majority of the world's population today is tormented by war, terrorism, and unrest. Conflict exists between nations regardless of our strong desire for world peace. Politicians continually babble about sustainable and enduring peace despite our history of virtually nonstop warfare and political turmoil.

Proponents of world peace have presented various theories for achieving global harmony and peace. I have briefly listed a few of the most popular theories.

Theories for World Peace

Imperial Peace

The Imperial Peace Theory, the oldest known theory for achieving world peace, proposes a universal conquest, wherein one nation conquers all other nations, leading to system-wide peace. This theory draws from historical examples such as the Bronze Age of Egypt, ancient Rome, medieval China, and the Inca nation. However, it is also viewed as detrimental, deplorable, and unachievable due to the inevitable fall of empires and the lack of necessary resources for maintaining worldwide supremacy.

Democratic Peace

Supporters of the Democratic Peace Theory argue that there is strong practical proof that democracies rarely wage war against each other. However, history shows that several wars have indeed taken place between democracies, which challenges the theory's absolute claims.

Capitalist Peace

In her essay "The Roots of War," Ayn Rand believed that capitalism created the longest period of peace in history, from the end of the Napoleonic Wars in 1815 to the outbreak of World War I in 1914. The Capitalism Peace Theory suggests that most of the major wars were perpetrated by the controlled economies against the freer ones, providing a unique perspective on the relationship between economic systems and peace.

Cobdenism

Advocates of Cobdenism maintain that free trade precludes a nation from becoming too self-sufficient (a requisite for extended conflict) and that international free trade would render war impossible. Removing tariffs and creating free trade would make war too costly for international businesses with production, research, and sales in many different nations, resulting in a powerful lobby opposed to global conflict.

Mutually Assured Destruction

The Mutually Assured Destruction Theory states that a full-scale nuclear war between two opposing nations would destroy both aggressors. In other words, the lethality of war reaches a point where it no longer presents an advantage for either side, thereby making war pointless.

The United Nations Charter

After World War II, the United Nations Charter set out to "save successive generations from the two scourges of war which twice in our lifetime has brought untold sorrow to mankind." The Charter emphasizes the acceptance of fundamental human rights, respect for international law, and a unity of independent countries to preserve world peace. The Charter recognizes "the inherent dignity and…the equal and inalienable rights of all members of the human family" as the foundation of freedom, justice, and "peace in the world."

Globalization

A trend has emerged in national politics wherein city-states and nation-states have united, and indications suggest that the international arena will ultimately follow suit. Nations like China, Italy, the United States, Australia, Germany, India, and Britain have combined into single nation-states, implying that continued globalization will create a world state.

Isolationism

The idea of Isolationism asserts that many nations can coexist in peace if they have each generated a firmer focus on their own internal affairs without attempting to impose restraint on other countries. Isolationism recommends not meddling in other nations' internal affairs while emphasizing protectionism and restriction of international trade and travel.

Non-Interventionism

Non-Interventionism encourages combining free trade (like Cobdenism) with political and military non-interference. Non-Interventionism should not be confused with Isolationism.

Self-Organized Peace

Proponents of Self-Organized Peace view world peace as the result of self-determined communal activities. This perspective empowers individuals and communities to take responsibility for preventing the institutionalization of power and fostering a culture of compassion and understanding.

Global Union of Scientists for Peace

The Global Union of Scientists for Peace, a coalition of prominent scientists and specialists, is a shining example of how scientific collaboration can be harnessed for the greater good. Their work to prevent war, terrorism, and nuclear proliferation and to promote safe, proven technologies inspires hope for a more peaceful future.

World Peace in Progress

The online World Peace in Progress project is designed to persuade the wealthiest, most intelligent, and most influential people to use their assets to eliminate global brutality and bloodshed. Its initiators regard liberty and free enterprise as a means of achieving world peace. Their World Peace Political Center brings together approximately 3,000 of the most powerful people on earth who want to create a legacy of world peace.

World religions often advocate for world peace, and each conveys a sincere desire to end global violence in its own way.

Bahá'í Faith

The focal objective of the Bahá'í Faith is establishing unity among the citizens of the world. Its founder, Bahá'u'lláh, affirms that "the fundamental purpose animating the Faith of God and His Religion is to safeguard the interests and promote the unity of the human race." The ultimate goal of the Bahá'í Faith is seen as a time of spiritual and social unity where humanity candidly connects with and cares for one another instead of merely tolerating each other.

Buddhism

Buddhists consider anger (and other negative states of mind) to be the root causes of war and fighting and believe that world peace will only be attained if we first establish peace within our minds. They believe people can live in peace and harmony by abandoning negative thoughts and emotions and fostering positive emotions such as love and compassion.

Buddhists have been integral to the movement toward world peace and have built Peace Pagodas to symbolize and inspire humanity to pursue world peace.

Hinduism

The essence of the ancient Hindu concept of Vasudha eka kutumbakam (the world is one family) is the belief that only corrupt minds see disharmony and opposition. Through greater wisdom, we become more inclusive and free from worldly illusions. World peace can only be achieved through the internal process of liberating ourselves from the man-made boundaries that separate the human race.

Jainism

A central concept of Jainism is compassion for all life, whether human or non-human. Human life is seen as a rare and exceptional opportunity to gain enlightenment.

Killing anyone for any reason is considered unthinkable and abhorrent. Jainism requires all participants to be vegetarian. Jainism'sJainism's view on World Peace is captured in the words of Virchand Gandhi: "May peace rule the universe; may peace rule in kingdoms and empires; may peace rule in states and in the lands of the potentates; may peace rule in the house of friends and may peace also rule in the house of enemies."

Sikhism

Peace comes from God, and there can be no worship without the performance of good deeds. Guru Nanak stressed that a Sikh should balance vocation, veneration, and charity and defend the rights of all creatures. They are persuaded to live with optimistic resilience and a concept of sharing, giving charitable donations, and working for the good of the community and others.

Nonviolence is a central concept of all Dharmic religions (Hinduism, Jainism, Buddhism and Sikhism).

Islam

Inner peace for Islam involves unequivocal faith and obedience to the only one God who is the source of Ultimate Peace. A common ancestry commencing with Adam and Eve serves as a reminder to quell the lethal ideology of ethnic superiority and enables people to live collectively on a common planet in peace and harmony.

"O mankind, we created you from a male and female and rendered you distinct peoples and tribes, that you may recognize and know one another. The best among you in the sight of God is the most righteous. Certainly, God is Omniscient, All-Aware." [22]

Knowing God brings true peace to the soul. When we have obtained peace within, we can develop genuinely peaceful relationships. Islam awaits the second coming of the prophet Isa (Jesus), when love and peace will make this world resemble paradise.

---

[22] Qur'an 49:13.

Judaism

World peace, or the notion of "repairing the world" (Tikkun Olam), is a fundamental principle of Judaism. Tikkun olam is accomplished through compassion and integrity, obedience to God's law, and moral persuasion. Jewish tradition awaits a future Messiah or "king appointed by God" to return the Jews to Israel, after which the world will experience unending worldwide peace and prosperity.

"And he shall judge between the nations and reprove many peoples, and they shall beat their swords into plowshares and their spears into pruning hooks; nation shall not lift the sword against nation, neither shall they learn war anymore." [23]

Christianity

Christian belief indicates that any semblance of world peace will only be achieved through the Word of God and by God's love, as exemplified in Jesus Christ's life. Obtaining

---

[23] Yeshayahu 2:4.

peace requires good works and forgiveness toward those who do wrong. However, a distinct difference in Christianity is that Christians do not expect to achieve worldwide peace until that peace is established upon the "new Earth" foretold in Revelation 21.

The Book of Matthew quotes Christ as saying: "Do not suppose that I have come to bring peace to the earth. I did not come to bring peace, but a sword. For I have come to turn a man against his father, a daughter against her mother, a daughter-in-law against her mother-in-law—a man's enemies will be the members of his own household." [24]

With such an ominous prospect looming in our lives, how do we find peace in our world? How do we achieve peace in the presence of fear? Man's ideology and the world's ways will continue to deliver chaos and confusion.

James addressed the cause of war and world conflict in a letter to Israel: "Where do wars and fightings among you come from?

---

[24] Matthew 10:34-36 (NET).

Don't they come from your pleasures that war in your members. You lust, and don't have. You kill, covet, and can't obtain. You fight and make war. Yet you don't have, because you don't ask. You ask, and don't receive, because you ask amiss, so that you may spent it for your pleasures." [25]

At the time James wrote this, the Jews were in open rebellion against Rome. They were fighting to preserve their religion and to procure their freedom. They had become divided into splinter groups and were fighting among themselves; all the while, they waged war against Egypt, Syria, and others. They were both slaughtering and being slaughtered. And so James posed the question, Doesn't war and fighting stem from your pursuit of pleasure, your passions, and your lust? [26]

The Jewish conflicts and aggressions were bred from their lust, which is the very same incentive for the wars that continue to distress and torment our world today. History is a repetitious recital of deliberate and

---

[25] James 4:1-3 (WEB).
[26] See James 4:1.

dissolute destruction of human life and personal property. A country covets another country's territory or property and forces its way of life on it through physical violence. Each nation will massacre, devastate, and demolish until one is overpowered. All the while, the politicians promise, and the people pray for world peace.

Peace has very different and distinct meanings and interpretations. The Greek word for peace denotes an end to or an absence of aggression between conflicting factions. It is simply the opposite of war and contention. The Hebrew word for peace, however, is far more comprehensive in meaning.

It has been commonly used as a greeting, "Peace be with you."

It also defines domestic peace between husband and wife and harmonious relations within families and among friends.

It also denotes peace of mind or serenity inspired by a proper relationship with God.

Due to these distinct definitions, our search for peace will lead us in very different directions. Society seeks a condition of world peace to end international hostilities and violence. However, sustainable world peace is achievable only within the conditions established by God.

Isaiah explained, "You will keep him in perfect peace, whose mind is stayed on you; because he trusts in you." [27] This perfect peace is achievable only through a belief in God. Inner peace and tranquility can be found in following correct gospel principles founded in Jesus Christ's teachings. Inner peace would then become familial peace, then communal peace, then national peace, and even world peace. But an unbelieving world would never be able to reconcile such an idea.

Peace in the Presence of Fear

Knowledge and understanding of spiritual matters determine whether Christians view the future with anxiety or anticipation—with fear or hope. The strength of our souls,

---

[27] Isaiah 26:3 (WEB).

not the circumstances of our lives, chases away the fear in our hearts and assures peace within. With a "perfect love" that "drives out fear," [28] Jesus consistently and persistently declares peace amid suffering and turmoil, present or future, expected or unexpected. Whether for individuals, families, communities, or churches, there are two critical ways in which we can become more spiritually strengthened: to better sustain our faith in troubling and turbulent times and to experience the peace that Jesus has promised us. One way is to prepare for what is ahead, and the other is to build on a sure and unshakeable foundation.

Preparation:

Our individual sustainability in the face of the coming challenges and difficulties depends less on the nature of those tumultuous circumstances or events and more on our own spiritual power to respond positively and effectively. We can view the predicted future events in terms of current trends, uncertain contingencies, or our own spiritual purposes.

---

[28] 1 John 4:18 (NET).

When we look at the future from the vantage point of current trends, we frequently see the future as an extension of the present. However, we cannot accurately determine what influences and activities will remain after today and continue to be influential in the future.

When we consider contingencies—possible but uncertain circumstances, such as earthquakes, tsunamis, fires, wars, and economic recessions—or, on the other hand, greater education and improved opportunities for work, the challenge becomes preparing ourselves to minimize the worst and accentuate the best, depending on which events actually transpire.

When we see the future in terms of our spiritual purposes, we attempt to design attitudes and ambitions that will shape our future and positively influence our choices. The challenge becomes properly identifying the attitudes that will survive troublesome times and challenging circumstances and establishing worthwhile objectives and ambitions for ourselves.

Whichever method we use to envision the future, our real purpose is to develop faith and confidence in the face of uncertainty and fear. We cannot predict the future, but we can prepare for it. Our faith and confidence will increase as we begin taking practical steps to lessen life's hazards and strengthen our own determination during difficult conditions.

Maintaining peace in the present and sustainable spiritual strength in the future is found in who we are, what we are capable of doing, and what we have done to minimize our risk. It is found in the strength of our principles and the grandeur of our goals. We should not merely wait for future events to unfold; we should think, work, and prepare to deal with them.

A Sure and Unshakeable Foundation:

Faith is a necessary part of our lives. Doubt and faith cannot exist in the same person at the same time. If we harbor doubts and fear, we will not have unshakeable confidence, and our faith will become ineffectual and unsustainable. If our faith is weak, it will not sustain us spiritually against the opposition, tribulation, and affliction that we will encounter as Christians.

The French philosopher and mathematician Blaise Pascal wrote: "There is a virtuous fear which is the effect of faith and a vicious fear which is the product of doubt and distrust. The former leads to hope as relying on God in whom we believe; the latter inclines to despair, as not relying upon God, in whom we do not believe. Persons of one character fear to lose God; those of the other character fear to find him." [29]

Two forces are battling to win our souls. Two opposing powers grapple continuously to gain our devotion. John foresaw the day when the just will come together in a deadly conflict, at Armageddon, against the forces of evil. These evil forces are busy preparing for that battle. They are arrayed against us, but we are not alone in our struggle. We have been promised help, aid, and

---

[29] Blaise Pascal (1623–62), in Tyron Edwards, *The New Dictionary of Thoughts*, p. 196.

assistance in achieving victory in the war against evil.

We are dual creatures with both a spiritual nature and a physical body. Just as light radiates from the sun and fills the solar system, there is a power and spirit and an influence radiating from God that fills the immensity of space. The influence that comes from God comes to us through our spiritual nature, not through the physical body. His help and support affect us through the spiritual senses and spiritual power. The power emanating from God is just as real as the light of the sun, and just as the physical body is sensitive to sunlight, our spiritual nature is sensitive and sensible to the light and power of God.

Job explains, "There is a spirit in man; and the inspiration of the Almighty giveth them understanding." [30] We are not merely physical beings; we are spiritual beings as well. Our knowledge of the meaning of life and our unique view of faith is displayed in Jesus' warning to his apostles: "Do not be afraid of

---

[30] Job 32:8 (KJV).

those who kill the body but cannot kill the soul. Instead, fear the one who is able to destroy both soul and body in hell." [31]

People who are spiritually asleep are in a sorrowful and unsustainable situation. They have no refuge, no promise of help, no power, and no strength to fight the forces of evil that seek our destruction. People cannot safely navigate the ups and downs and dangers of life without the help of the Lord. This is why he pleads with us to constantly seek him.

King David declared: "If I ascend up into heaven, you are there. If I make my bed in Sheol, behold, you are there!" [32] By the presence and power of his Spirit, God is everywhere. In the midst of the trials and turmoil that surround us, we need to turn to this source of strength to sustain us and support us in weathering the approaching storms of life. There is an abundance of power available to everyone who sincerely and honestly seeks to make themselves strong enough to succeed and attain victory over the

---

[31] Matthew 10:28 (NET).
[32] Psalms 139:8 (WEB).

devil and all his schemes against the human soul. Herein rests the efficacy of Christ's instruction to "be not troubled." [33]

The promise of peace is extended only to those who believe in God and obey his law and commandments. Isaiah described the decadence and depravity of certain leaders, then added: "The wicked are like the troubled sea; for it can't rest, and its waters cast up mire and dirt. There is no peace, says my God, to the wicked." [34]

The wicked receive no peace, and their unrighteous activities cheat the rest of us out of our promise of peace. World conflicts are usually instigated by a small but powerful minority who thoughtlessly and ruthlessly bring suffering and sorrow to millions of innocent people.

The innocent victims of oppressors have always prayed for peace. They have demonstrated, rioted, and even died in an effort to bring an end to violence and hostility.

---

[33] Matthew 24:6 (KJV).
[34] Isaiah 57: 20, 21 (WEB).

Sustainable world peace will be achieved only through Jesus giving peace to his disciples and "not as the world does." [35]

Emerson wrote, "Nothing can bring you peace but yourself; nothing can bring you peace but the triumph of principles." [36] The principles that will ultimately bring peace are found in the gospel of Jesus Christ. Rejecting Christ and his teachings creates insecurity, inner conflict, and contention. Peace comes through absolute submission to the Prince of peace.

When we accept Jesus, we will find peace. Jesus taught us that we would have trouble and suffering in the world, [37] but that we could find peace in a world of conflict if we accept his great gift and invitation: "Come to me, all you who are weary and burdened, and I will give you rest. Take my yoke on you, and learn from me, because I am gentle and humble

---

in heart, and you will find rest for your souls." [38]

A great writer named Fenelon said, "Peace does not dwell in outward things, but within the soul; we may preserve it in the midst of the bitterest pain, if our will remains firm and submissive. Peace in this life springs from acquiescence, not in an exemption from suffering." [39]

This peace protects us from a world in conflict. Knowing that God lives and loves us pacifies the troubled heart. Faith in God and his Son, Jesus Christ, is the key to sustainable world peace. Only this will bring us lasting peace.

Faith in Jesus is the foundation of peace and the greatest defense against fear, hopelessness, and depression. Just before Jesus took on the suffering of Gethsemane and Golgotha, he blessed his apostles: "Peace I leave with you, my peace I give to you: I do not give it as the world does. Do not let your hearts

---

[38] Matthew 11:28, 29 (NET).
[39] Source Unknown.

be distressed or lacking in courage." [40] With unshakeable faith built upon the foundation of Christ, we, too, can know this peace and witness with Paul that "God did not give us a Spirit of fear but of power and love and self-control." [41]

---

[40] John 14:27 (NET).
[41] 2 Timothy 1:7 (NET).

CHAPTER FOUR

THE REAL OIL CRISIS

When a youth group from a local church was asked what one question they would most like to ask Jesus about his second coming, three particular questions came up repeatedly. As we might expect, "When will it happen?" was the most asked question. The second question varied in wording but contained essentially a similar idea: "What will life be like before he comes?" Not surprisingly, the third most frequently asked question was, "What can I do to be ready?" This question about our individual spiritual preparedness is not just a matter of curiosity but a call to action. We would probably all love to know the answers to the first two questions, but the answer to the third question seems significantly more pressing and essential.

Malachi portrays the second coming of Jesus Christ in his paradoxical phrase, "the great and terrible day of the Lord." [42] We must wonder how a day could be both great and terrible simultaneously. The future shoulders some outrageous and appalling events—wars, murders, wickedness, violent storms, great earthquakes, floods, food shortages, sickness, and disease. Alternatively, the future will also convey many events that make it a great day—the Kingdom of God will devour all other kingdoms, [43] and Jesus will return to separate the wheat from the weeds. [44]

So, what determines whether it's a great day or a terrible day for us individually? How does the faithful Christian look toward an uncertain future with faith and anxious anticipation instead of with fear and apprehension? The answer lies in our faith. Whether we see Jesus' return as a great day or a terrible day depends mainly on how

---

[42] Malachi 4:5 (NET).
[43] See Daniel 2:44.
[44] See Matthew 13:30.

sustainable our faith and spirituality are today. If we want to be ready for the future, we must strengthen our faith in Jesus Christ. Our faith can transform uncertainty into hope and fear into anticipation.

After encouraging his disciples not to be alarmed, the Lord mentioned a common proverb in the Holy Land: "Learn this parable from the fig tree: Whenever its branch becomes tender and puts out its leaves, you know that summer is near." [45]

Since the fig tree is one of the last trees to put forth leaves, it became common in the Middle East to say that if leaves were starting on the fig tree, summer would arrive, and the cold weather would be over. Jesus compared the leaves of the fig tree to the signs of the times: "So also you, when you see these things happening, know that he is near, right at the door…Watch out! Stay alert! For you do not know when the time will come." [46] Jesus has counseled us to watch for the signs of the times. Like the leaves of the fig tree, certain

---

[45] Mark 13:28 (NET).
[46] Mark 13: 29, 33 (NET).

specific signs will indicate that his coming is near. This call to vigilance should make us feel alert and attentive, always watching for the signs of his coming.

Much of what the future holds may be unpleasant. Some of what awaits the world because of its wickedness is dreadful and deeply depressing. But God has given us a knowledge of the future—even of the terrible events—so that when they occur, we will recognize them as the fulfillment of God's word. We will see them as proof that his word is all being fulfilled.

The parable of the ten virgins evokes a brilliant portrayal of a Middle Eastern wedding. George Mackie, a Christian minister who lived much of his life in the Holy Land, described a Palestinian wedding ceremony with the following rich and revealing imagery:

"Oriental marriages," he wrote, "usually take place in the evening.... The whole attention is turned to the public arrival of the bridegroom to receive the bride prepared for him and waiting in the house among her female attendants....

"As the hours drag on their topics of conversation become exhausted, and some of them grow tired and fall asleep. There is nothing more to be done, and everything is in readiness for the reception of the bridegroom, when the cry is heard outside announcing his approach.

"The bridegroom meanwhile is absent, spending the day at the house of one of his relatives. There, soon after sunset, that is between seven and eight o'clock, his male friends begin to assemble…. The time is occupied with light refreshments, general conversation and the recitation of poetry in praise of the two families chiefly concerned and of the bridegroom in particular. After all have been courteously welcomed and their congratulations received, the bridegroom, about eleven o'clock, intimates his wish to set out. Flaming torches are then held aloft by special bearers, lit candles are handed at the door to each visitor as he goes out, and the procession sweeps slowly along toward the house where the bride and her female attendants are waiting. A great crowd has meanwhile assembled on the balconies, garden-walls, and flat roofs of the houses on each side of the road…. The bridegroom is the centre of interest. Voices are heard whispering, 'There he is! There he is!' From time to time women raise their voices in the peculiar shrill, wavering shriek by which joy is expressed at marriages and other times of family and public rejoicing. The sound is heard at a great distance, and is repeated by other voices in advance of the procession, and thus intimation is given of the approach half an hour or more before the marriage escort arrives…. As the house is approached the excitement increases, the bridegroom's pace is quickened, and the alarm is raised in louder tones and more repeatedly, 'He is coming, he is coming!'

"Before he arrives, the maidens in waiting come forth with lamps and candles a short distance to light up the entrance, and do honour to the bridegroom and the group of relatives and intimate friends around him. These pass into the final rejoicing and the marriage supper; the others who have discharged their duty in accompanying him to the door, immediately disperse, and the door is shut." [47]

In Jesus' day and time, olive oil was used to fuel the small clay or brass lamps people carried outside at night to light their steps. Outfitted with a short wick, the lamps were small enough to fit in the palm of a hand and obviously held only a minimal amount of oil. They could burn for about an hour before going out. It seems that olive oil is the principal part of this parable.

So, just what does olive oil represent? Olive oil represents the Holy Spirit, whose influence is often portrayed as burning and fire. The Bible speaks of being baptized with "the Holy Spirit and with fire." [48] The Spirit of God is a source of light and truth, and olive oil, as far as the parable is concerned, denotes the light and power of the Holy Spirit.

The ten virgins represent Christ's followers, not the world's general population. All ten of them, both the wise and the foolish,

---

[47] George Mackie, *Bible Manners and Customs* (New York: Fleming H. Revell, 1898), 123-26.
[48] Matthew 3:11 (NET).

had accepted the invitation to the wedding supper. They were not pagans or heathens. They were the ones who had been invited to participate in that all-important symbolic event. But half of them were foolishly unprepared for the critical event that would affect their future.

Consider how the five wise virgins were different from the five foolish ones. All of them were virgins, and all of them had brought their lamps. The only difference was the extra olive oil the wise virgins brought. When we recognize the imagery employed in this parable, then the message becomes apparent. We all need an additional portion of the Holy Spirit to be prepared for Christ's coming. Jesus has given us this parable as a special warning.

In the darkest hours of our lives, heaven offers joy in exchange for our weariness. It is often difficult to distinguish between the wise and the foolish in the daylight hours, but the midnight shadows will reveal our wisdom. At the darkest hour, Christ will come, and there will be no more time to prepare. The foolish virgins wanted the wise to share the oil they had brought with them, but sustainable spirituality cannot simply be handed to us. Faith, obedience, and a knowledge of God cannot simply be given away. Each of us must obtain for ourselves the necessary oil to provide us with enough light to endure the darkness.

In the parable, olive oil could be purchased at the market. In real life, spiritual oil is collected one drop at a time through Christ-like living. Church attendance, prayer, witnessing to others, studying God's word, and every act of devotion add a drop of oil to our lamps. Righteous thoughts and acts of kindness add to the supply of oil we can use at midnight to refuel our dimming lamps.

Seeing how imperative it is to have the Holy Spirit with us in troubling times, the real oil crisis of our time is not what we see at the gas pumps. The single most significant factor to sustainable spirituality is to live so that we can have the influence and guidance of the Holy Spirit to witness Christ's truth and help us avoid deception. The parable of the ten virgins teaches us how to become spiritually sustainable by living so that we will feel the influence of the Holy Spirit to give us testimony and guide us through the darkness ahead.

The Holy Spirit is our close companion when we live the gospel of Christ. Obeying Jesus' teachings is the only way to ensure our lamps are filled with oil. Christ has given each one of us a lamp. Whether there is oil in our lamp is up to us. If we follow Jesus' teachings and example, we will have an adequate supply of the necessary oil to light our way through the darkness. We cannot borrow from others. We can only purchase oil from the eternal supply offered at the fountain of truth, our Savoir, Jesus Christ. Whether or not we have oil in our lamps is solely determined by our individual faithfulness to him.

CHAPTER FIVE

ENDING WORLD HUNGER

We find ourselves in a time of unprecedented uncertainty. The United States is grappling with unemployment not seen since the Great Depression. Families are facing hunger and deprivation at levels reminiscent of Lyndon Johnson's war on poverty in the 1960s. Our nations are deeply divided politically, economically, and socially. The immediate future offers little hope for ending world hunger. The urgency of these global issues cannot be overstated.

Solving starvation and poverty is one enormous stumbling block to achieving a sustainable world environment. According to the Brundtland Commission report, *Our*

Common Future, poverty is a source of environmental degradation. The report indicates that "poverty is a major cause and effect of global environmental problems. It is therefore futile to attempt to deal with environmental problems without a broader perspective that encompasses the factors underlying world poverty and international inequality." [49] Populations in poverty rely heavily on local ecosystems for fundamental needs such as nutrition, medicine, and general well-being.

The grim and horrifying pictures of starving humanity in India, Africa, and many other nations throughout the world reveal the scrawny limbs, the bloated stomachs, and the skeletal faces of these poor, unfortunate masses suffering from the lack of adequate food to nourish and build up their bodies.

As horrific as this deprivation is, an even ghastlier famine was predicted by the Old Testament Prophet Amos, who forewarned:

---

[49] The Brundtland Commission Report, *Our Common Future*.

"Behold, the days come, saith the Lord God, that I will send a famine in the land, not a famine of bread, nor a thirst for water, but of hearing the words of the Lord:

"And they shall wander from sea to sea, and from the north even to the east, they shall run to and fro to seek the word of the Lord, and shall not find it." [50]

The sight of millions starving themselves of the fully sustaining divine food that could render them spiritually strong and wholesome with a vital and living faith is no less tragic! On the one hand, we witness the mortal homicide brought on humanity through greed and avarice; on the other, we see the self-inflicted curse of spiritual suicide.

Throughout my lifetime, I have been indoctrinated to accept the claim that our world has become overpopulated. A recent United Nations International Conference on Population and Development held in Cairo, Egypt, centered its debate around what it calls "sustainable growth." Not many people in the

---

[50] Amos 8:11,12 (KJV).

world's developed nations would argue against such a socially acceptable phrase despite the Biblical command to "Be fruitful and multiply! Fill the earth and subdue it!" [51]

In the September 1994 issue of Forbes Magazine, a carefully thought-out editorial maintains that people are an asset, not a liability to our planet. It candidly pronounces the widely accepted premise as unbelievable that a decrease in population growth is necessary for economic development. The editorial convincingly declares that "free people don't exhaust resources; they create them." [52]

Furthermore, a U.S. News and World Report article maintains that the earth can produce food for a population of at least eighty billion! This is eight times the estimated ten billion people who will populate the planet by 2050 A.D. Another study suggests that the earth could feed as many as one thousand

---

[51] Genesis 1:28 (NET).
[52] Forbes Magazine, 12 September 1994, p. 25.

billion people through further developed and enhanced scientific techniques. [53]

Those who argue for sustainable growth need more vision and faith. Spiritual sustainability comes from being rooted and grounded in the gospel of Jesus Christ. When we are settled in the faith, securely fastened to principles of truth, we will become nourished by the word of God. We do not need to starve ourselves by seeking truth in the false ideas, philosophies, and vagaries of a godless humanity. The Christian foundation for truth has Jesus Christ as the chief cornerstone. [54]

Every builder knows that a good building with a bad foundation is useless and dangerous. John Stott explains, "If the stability of buildings depends largely on their foundations, so does the stability of human lives. The search for personal security is a primal instinct, but many fail to find it today. Old familiar landmarks are being obliterated. Moral absolutes which were once thought to

---

[53] *Ten Billion for Dinner, Please.* U.S. News and World Report, 12 September 1994, pp. 57-60.
[54] See Ephesians 2:19-20.

be eternal are being abandoned." [55] Our house of faith is only as secure as the foundation it is built on. When human support fails us, our hearts must be riveted on the things of the Spirit, those internal realities that provide meaning, perspective, and the necessary sustenance for all that matters.

A Jewish tradition claims that during the early stages of the construction of the Jewish temple, the builders mistakenly discarded the cornerstone. Centuries later, Jesus spoke of people disregarding him and his message. "Have you never read in the scriptures; 'The stone the builders rejected has become the cornerstone. This is from the Lord, and it is marvelous in our eyes.'?" [56]

The challenge for those who aspire to Christian discipleship is to build our lives on Christ and construct a house of faith where his Spirit can reside. There is safety only in Christ. There is security only in his word and through his infinite and eternal power. But with so many babbling voices enticing us into

---

[55] Stott, John, *Life in Christ*, p. 22.
[56] Matthew 21:42, (NET) compare Psalm 118:22-23, Acts 4:11.

forbidden paths, how do we know the Way, live the Truth, and gain that life abundantly offered to us?

In our overly complex world, people eagerly sell solutions to all our troubles. People gorge themselves on self-improvement programs, internet blogs, magazine articles, seminars, courses, and workshops. They eat up the idea of self-discovery, learning who they are and what they can achieve. They eagerly devour programs that foster personal worth and self-esteem. They gobble down the philosophy that the answer to their personal problems lies deep within and that the key to understanding and correcting their attitudes and actions lies buried deep in their past. They feed on the popular teaching that their problems are a product of how people mistreated them and that they must work through those relationships to become whole. With all of this, they are still starving for truth.

Underlying this "pursuit of excellence" is a very revealing philosophy that deep-seated problems can only be solved by professional therapists and counselors and that feasting on the word of God, studying the Bible, praying, forgiving others, repenting, and making righteous choices based on Christ's gospel are all too simplistic and inadequate in dealing with today's complex challenges.

In his eye-opening book, *The Screwtape Letters,* C. S. Lewis portrays an archdevil named Screwtape training his nephew, Wormwood, how to deceive Christians. "The real trouble about the set your patient is living in," explains Screwtape, "is that it is merely Christian. They all have individual interests, of course, but the bond remains mere Christianity. What we want, if men become Christians at all, is to keep them in the state of mind I call 'Christianity And.' You know—Christianity and the Crisis, Christianity and the New Psychology, Christianity and the New Order, Christianity and Faith Healing, Christianity and Psychical Research, Christianity and Vegetarianism, Christianity and Spelling Reform. If they must be Christians, let them at least be Christians with a difference. Substitute for the faith itself some Fashion with a Christian colouring. Work on their horror of the Same Old Thing." [57]

---

[57] C.S. Lewis, *The Screwtape Letters*, pp. 115-116.

The devil doesn't require us to lie, cheat or steal. All he needs is for us to ignore, lessen, and devalue the power and significance of the teachings of Jesus Christ.

Our expanding world of information and technology challenges Christians worldwide to feast on the fundamentals and the basic, simple teachings of the gospel. Discoveries will continue to relieve human suffering and free humanity from many of life's struggles, but some things will never change. Some things are resolved only through divine intervention.

Paul taught that in Christ, "all the fullness of deity lives in bodily form, and you have been filled in him, who is the head over every ruler and authority."[58]

Too often, we underestimate the magnitude of Jesus Christ's love and power in re-creating and renewing the human personality. The Spirit of God is incredibly therapeutic. God's love extends far beyond any earthly substitute. In seeking solutions to life's

---

[58] Colossians 2:9-10 (NET).

problems, we should consider the word of God and the guidance of the Holy Spirit as seriously as we consider humanity's ideas and standards.

Our preoccupation with success and excellence is commendable, to a degree, in that it helps us focus on the tasks at hand and assists us in being more effective. But we need perspective. I don't diminish the value of personal achievement and growth or the striving for excellence as long as part of our striving includes the deep desire to find God and accept the procedures he offers to enlarge our lives and souls.

Modern pursuits of excellence often become an attempt to please or impress other people. In the end, other people are not our judges, and giving too much attention to their positive or negative judgments can undermine our relationship with God and our development of sound Christian values.

We should have grand goals and do what we can to achieve them. But our personal goals should be in harmony with God's grander purpose for us. As my wife often reminds me, "Do you want what you want, or do you want something better?"

The power of life and salvation is in Christ. His grace can heal us if we yield, submit, and rely on Him. Jesus came to change human nature. On the other hand, we want to solve our problems in our own way. We renew or remake our personality through some personal behavior modification plan. We work on our flaws and weaknesses for extended periods, then advance to another.

Our efforts certainly have merit as they encourage us to eliminate our character flaws. Benjamin Franklin used just such a system for self-improvement. But sometimes, it's like trying to simultaneously hold a hundred ping-pong balls underwater. Eventually, some will pop up out of the water, and more will find their way to the surface in attempting to re-submerge those.

Our sins and shortcomings are similar, making it impractical and even impossible to change our lives that way. If you want to get your life in order, consider an alternative approach—ask God to make you a new creature in Christ, to give you a clean heart and an educated conscience.

God's way is so much more effective, so much more satisfying, and so much less frustrating. He asks us to be born again, to have our natures changed so that we will not desire to engage in our old sinful ways. He asks us to acknowledge our weaknesses and human limitations and to demonstrate faith in his power to renew and refine us.

We should do our best to overcome bad habits but also lean on that arm that is mighty to save. Then, we will notice changes in our nature. We can strengthen our resolve with the following three steps:

1. Feast on the words of the Lord.

The scriptures contain the words of Christ. Reading and studying them is how we hear the voice of the Master. The Bible has been written and endorsed to bring us to Christ and to establish us in his doctrine. When we become serious students of the Bible, striving to understand and apply scriptural precepts and principles, we will readily see the hand of

God in our lives, and we can better discern the handiwork of Satan. We become better equipped to sift through the sordid and further prepared to distinguish the divine from the diabolical and the sacred from the secular.

The word of God helps us recognize and refute teachings and ideas that take us on intellectual and philosophical detours. It allows us to cut through false notions and discard counterfeit philosophies that may seem pleasing to the human intellect but are, in reality, damaging to our spiritual sustainability. It allows us to become grounded and settled in truth, anchored to the Lord's word and built on the rock of Christ.

2. Share this spiritual food.

Spiritual power accompanies those who share the Lord's word with people starving for spiritual sustenance. Human philosophy, however pleasantly stated or however admirable and appropriate it may appear, cannot connect with the soul in the same way the doctrines of Christ can. If we teach the gospel of Christ with the power and persuasion of the Holy Spirit, others will be turned to Christ.

3. Trust in God.

There is a power in Christ to calm the seas and the storms of the human heart, to mend the hurt of broken and defeated souls.

There is a power in Christ to assume the obligation of our sins, for we cannot remit our own sins any more than we can resurrect ourselves. We are truly saved by the grace of our God.

When we are contaminated by sin and enveloped in the spiritual darkness that follows transgression, it is often hard to see how to disentangle ourselves. Even when we are brought to know the way of life and truth, we may find it difficult to follow. The fact that we have lost virtue may evidence a weakness of character, making it hard for us to apply the principles by which we can regain innocence and acquire spiritual strength.

Nevertheless, the pangs of guilt and remorse of conscience that sinners feel may awaken a desire for righteousness in us. With a new determination to do right, coupled with the mercy and power that God extends to those who genuinely desire to come unto him, we can be renewed to a state of purity and power in Christ.

We must learn to trust in him more, rely on him more, and surrender our burdens to him more. We must be willing to seek that grace or enabling power that will make up the difference, that sacred power that makes all the difference!

Our challenge to discern good from evil, light from darkness, and virtue from vice includes discerning between things that matter most and those of little or no real value. Disputatious ideas steal our time and attention. Dissonant voices absorb our interest. We should be more discriminating concerning our time, interest, and attention. Some things matter more than others and the thing that matters most is the knowledge and testimony of Jesus. "For no one can lay any other foundation than what is being laid, which is Jesus Christ." [59]

God will assist us with our problems quite differently from the world's solutions. If you thirst for excellence, the world will offer you a glass of water. You can drink it, get on with your life, career, and family responsibilities, and make your way in the world. But Jesus Christ can offer you a well of water, a spring of eternal life, and you need never thirst again. This water is essential to our spiritual sustainability.

Living Water to Quench Spiritual Thirst

Several years ago, a local newspaper printed a story of a Boy Scout in Arizona who died from heat exhaustion after his water ran out. The Scout troop had not counted on three days of record-breaking temperatures in the Arizona desert. While searching for water in the 112-degree heat, one Scout fainted just 100 yards from the Colorado River. He died a short time later. The unexpected loss of this young boy's life, the anguish of his fellow Scouts, and

---

[59] 1 Corinthians 3:11(NET).

the heartbreak of his sorrowing parents all contribute to making this such a distressing tragedy.

I have wondered many times since about those who are dying spiritually from a thirst for living water. Perhaps someone just a hundred yards from living water is suffering spiritual exhaustion or dying of spiritual thirst.

The newspaper article followed the tragic account of the Boy Scout's demise with a list of survival tips for desert hikers. The same techniques apply to surviving the spiritual deserts we encounter in life.

1. Take adequate water with you. Drink at least a gallon of water a day and more during sweltering weather.

How much spiritual water do we have available during a spiritual crisis? Can we stave off spiritual exhaustion with just a sip from a cup, or do we need to drink deeply from the words of the Bible or the power of prayer when things become particularly hot?

2. Carry all your water with you. Don't depend on natural sources along the trail.

We must become spiritually self-reliant. We must all carry our own living water with us, guided by the light within. If we do not take this water ourselves, we may not survive. We must prepare ourselves spiritually for any difficult time ahead.

3. Always hike with an experienced guide, one who is familiar with the area.

As Christians, we have an infallible guide: the Holy Spirit. We will hear this direction in our minds and hearts as we pray for guidance and bearing.

If we pray fervently, follow the directions of our Guide, and read our survival manual, the Bible, every day (and more when the temperatures are hot and temptations are strong), then this living water will quench our spiritual thirst and save our spiritual lives.

The Lord unconditionally loves us despite our weaknesses, imperfections, wrong choices, and mistakes. He offers us living water while we suffer a parched thirst. Will we fill our buckets from the well of living water at church? Will we drink deeply from the messages of living water in the Bible, or will we take a sip from the cup and travel on?

We must quench our spiritual thirst at the fountain of living waters, fill our pitchers, canteens, and vessels, and carry the living water with us through the deserts of life. And then, we should share that water with anyone along the way who is suffering spiritual thirst because they don't know where to find this living water.

Jehovah acknowledged ancient Israel's double sin, declaring, "My people have committed a double wrong: they have rejected me, the fountain of life-giving water, and they have dug cisterns for themselves, cracked cisterns which cannot even hold water." [60] Rejecting or ignoring God is a serious matter. We must not turn a deaf ear to his divine direction.

The Lord is the Way. When we refuse his message, we descend a broad road headed

____

[60] Jeremiah 2:13 (NET).

for destruction. Conversely, when we follow his guidance, we embark on a narrow path leading to life and fulfillment. Each step taken in faith is illuminated by his light, helping us navigate the challenges and trials ahead. Though the journey may be fraught with obstacles, we find strength in our unwavering trust in Him.

In moments of doubt or despair, it is essential to remember his promises—that He will never leave or forsake us. With every prayer offered and every ounce of hope nurtured within our hearts, we grow closer to understanding his divine purpose for our lives.

We must not be swayed by the distractions of this world but instead cling tightly to the truth found in scripture. By immersing ourselves in his word and surrounding ourselves with those who share our faith, we nourish our spirits and fortify ourselves against temptation.

The call to walk with the Lord is an invitation filled with grace; each moment spent in communion deepens our relationship with him. As we align our desires with his will, we discover true peace amid chaos and joy, even during trials.

The Lord is a beacon guiding us through dark times into a future radiant with hope. We should commit to seeking Him diligently and trusting fully as He leads us on this sacred journey toward eternity.

The Lord is the Truth. When we snub his teachings, we wander in ignorance. We become lost in a maze of confusion, seeking answers in places that can only lead to more questions. The light he offers is a beacon, guiding us through the darkness of our own misunderstandings and fears. In embracing his wisdom, we find clarity and purpose.

To live by the Truth is to walk on a path illuminated by love, compassion, and understanding. Each step toward acknowledging the Lord's presence brings us closer to fulfillment. As we align ourselves with divine principles, we are empowered to shed negativity internally and externally and embrace a life of kindness and respect for all of God's creation.

In moments of doubt or despair, turning back to this sacred guidance can rekindle hope within us. It reminds us that even amid life's trials, there lies an omnipresent truth waiting for recognition—a truth that assures us of grace when we stumble and comfort when sorrow strikes.

When we heed his words, we allow our hearts to remain steadfast in seeking Him, the ultimate reality—the source of joy flowing endlessly into our lives. his words inspire action rooted deeply in faith that transcends mere belief and becomes a living testimony born from Him who embodies eternal wisdom.

The Lord is the Light. When we forsake him, we walk in darkness. When we turn away from his guiding presence, shadows envelop our path, and uncertainty clouds our vision. In moments of despair, we may stumble and lose our way, but his light remains within reach even in the depths of darkness. If we seek Him with a sincere heart and open spirit, He will illuminate our lives again.

In his light, we find hope, clarity, and purpose. It offers warmth to the cold places within us and dispels the fears that grip our hearts.

We should cherish this divine illumination, letting it guide each decision and action as we navigate life's trials and tribulations. Then, when the storms threaten to obscure our sight, we will remain anchored in faith. Ultimately, it is through Him that we discover direction and peace amidst the chaos.

The Lord is the Life. When we refuse to unite with his will, we are courting spiritual death. When we choose our path over his guidance, we may find ourselves lost in the shadows of despair and confusion. His plans for us are rooted in love and purpose, but it requires our surrender to his divine wisdom. In times of challenge, turning away from his light can lead us into a wilderness of doubt and fear.

Embracing the Lord's will allows us to tap into a source of strength that surpasses understanding. It nurtures our spirits and illuminates our hearts, guiding us toward fulfillment and joy. In this journey toward unity with Him, we discover the transformative power of love—a love that heals wounds, bridges divides, and fosters reconciliation within ourselves and among communities.

In moments where resistance arises within us—the urge to cling tightly to control or pursue fleeting satisfactions—we must remind ourselves that the essence of existence thrives when surrendered wholly to God's plan. Only by embracing his vision for our lives can we fully experience the richness of spiritual abundance He so graciously offers.

The Lord is the Fountain of Living Waters. When we forsake him, we stop the flow of living water that would quench the world's thirst. In our longing for fulfillment, we often seek solace in fleeting pleasures and temporary distractions, but these wells are dry and cannot satisfy our deep thirst. When we turn away from the source of true life, we become parched and weary, struggling to find meaning without Him.

Returning to the Lord, we can reawaken that flow of living water—an endless supply of grace, hope, and purpose. This divine refreshment nourishes our souls and empowers us to extend that same hydration to those around us who are desperate for relief.

We become conduits of his love and compassion, sharing this living water with a world yearning for truth and healing. In moments of doubt or despair, may we remember where our sustenance truly lies: in the arms of the One who promises never to leave nor forsake us.

Digging our reservoirs will not relieve our parched and scorched souls. Human-made reservoirs will be insufficient and undersupplied. They cannot hold the spiritual water that would deliver us from the afflictions of the future.

Our supply of living water is only in question if we shut off the flow ourselves. The Lord promises, "I will pour water upon him that is thirsty, and floods upon the dry ground: I will pour my spirit upon thy seed, and my blessing upon thine offspring." [61] The source of living water is abundant and full. We can drink all we need and still have enough to share

----

[61] Isaiah 44:3 (KJV).

with everyone around us. This living water nurtures our spirits and revitalizes our souls, offering comfort in times of trouble and hope amidst despair. It flows freely, unrestrained by boundaries or limitations, reminding us that generosity begets abundance. As we quench our thirst with this divine essence, we become vessels of its grace, pouring out kindness and compassion to those parched in spirit.

With every sip taken from this source, may we cultivate gratitude for the incredible gift we've been given, our hearts overflowing as we share not just with words but through actions that reflect the warmth and light of this sacred water.

CHAPTER SIX

RENEWABLE ENERGY

Energy consumed at insignificant rates compared to its supply and with governable environmental effects is sustainable energy. Technologies that support sustainable energy include renewable energy sources, such as hydroelectricity, solar energy, wind energy, wave power, geothermal energy, and other technologies designed to improve energy efficiency.

Climate change concerns, coupled with high oil prices and increased government support, are enhancing interest in the sustainable energy industry. Moving toward increased sustainable energy will require changes not only in the way energy is supplied but also in how it is used, reducing the amount of energy required to deliver various goods or services.

Energy efficiency and renewable energy are the twin pillars of sustainable energy. Creating sustainable energy will require providing energy that meets the needs of "the present without compromising the ability of future generations to meet their own needs." [62] The solution is finding "sustainable energy sources and more efficient means of converting and utilizing energy."[63]

Life is too short to spend our energy getting caught up in unimportant causes. Imagine devoting your time, talents, and energy to a cause you later learn is fruitless. It's like climbing a ladder only to discover it is leaning against the wrong wall. Some things in life matter more than others.

Instead of squandering our time and energy on the trivial concerns of the world, we must find a way to sustain our spiritual energy

---

[62] Renewable Energy and Efficiency Partnership (British).
[63] *Sustainable Energy* by J. W. Tester, et al., from MIT Press.

in the storms of derision and through the troubling times to come. As Christians, we need to be able to distinguish between what is crucial and what is merely convenient. We need to be able to discern between the fundamental and the fleeting. We must sift through our time's sordid and secondary causes and focus our efforts and energy on the greater good. Such a substantial effort will require a significant and sustainable source of power to support our undertaking. It will require that we become energetic and energized Christians.

Is our commitment to Christ fully charged with enough power and energy to withstand the adversity of our times? How do we gain sufficient energy to dedicate our lives to continuously following Christ and living consistently by our Christian beliefs and values? From what source of power do we draw the energy to resist Satan's temptations? Do we have the energy to walk as Jesus walked when the road becomes too harsh to travel? We can find and sustain all the renewable energy we need through the power of the Son!

Energized Christians put Christ first in their lives. Our egos tend to want to place us at the center of the universe, where we expect everyone else to conform to our wants and desires. Our spiritual nature does not concur with such a mistaken notion. The central station of our lives belongs to God. Instead of expecting him to conform to our wishes, we should bring our lives into harmony with his will.

Energized Christians make a consorted effort toward a total commitment to the cause of Christianity. We don't simply climb onto the strait and narrow path and stand there chit-chatting with each other about how fortunate we are. We perform the acts of Christianity that the gospel of Christ requires of us.

Energized Christians move forward with a clarity of faith, a love of God, and a resoluteness in Christ. Having the energy to walk as Jesus walked means we obey the two great commandments: to love God and our neighbors. The first great commandment is: "Love the Lord your God with all your heart, with all your soul, and with all your mind." [64] To properly love God, we must be willing to do what he asks of us. Our actions, more than

---

[64] Matthew 22:37 (NET).

our words, will always reflect who we are and what we believe.

Energized Christians focus on their distinct and particular purpose and never look back on their past problems or transgressions. To us, the past is nothing more than an indication of our growth and our value in God's eyes.

When a certain man approached Jesus, he said, "I will follow you, Lord, but first let me say goodbye to my family." Jesus told him, "No one who puts his hand to the plow and looks back is fit for the kingdom of God." [65] Digging a straight furrow requires the person plowing to keep his eyes fixed on a distinct point before him. If he looks back to see where he has been, he loses his reference point and increases his chance of drifting and plowing a crooked, uneven furrow. A more modern metaphor might be trying to drive a car while looking behind you to see what the kids in the backseat are doing. It would be an extremely dangerous and perhaps even deadly practice.

---

[65] Luke 9:61, 62 (NET).

Energized Christians listen to the Holy Spirit, persistently pursue its power and guidance, and pray for the energy and strength to conquer challenges and trials. Our hearts are set upon the things of heaven, and that is where our treasure will also be.

Energized Christians strengthen other believers and non-believers. We are eager to share the source of our spiritual energy and the purveyor of our happiness and hope. At the end of his life, Patrick Henry remarked, "I have now disposed of all my property to my family…. There is one thing more I wish I could give them, and that is the Christian religion…. If they had that, and I had not given them one shilling, they would have been rich, and if they had not that, and I had given them all the world, they would be poor." [66]

Energized Christians put their beliefs into action. We anxiously perform excellent and noble deeds. We have ambition and desire, and we do all we can do to advance the work of God on Earth.

---

[66] *The New Dictionary of Thoughts* [Garden City, New York: Standard Book Co., 1961], 561.

Energized Christians love one another and care for refugees, orphans, widows, or anyone needing assistance. This love and care are not just words but actions that demonstrate our commitment to living a Christian life.

Energized Christians believe in a living God. Before he crossed the Jordan River, Joshua called the children of Israel, saying, "Come here and listen to the words of the Lord your God.... This is how you will know the living God is among you." [67]

Challenged by the giant Goliath, the young shepherd David courageously said to those near him, "…Who is this uncircumcised Philistine, that he defies the armies of the living God?" [68] Jeremiah also called the Lord "the living God and the everlasting King." [69]

Energized Christians are completely convinced of a living God. Our only question is: Am I dedicated and committed to being an energetic, energized, and "living" Christian?

---

[67] Joshua 3:9, 10 (NET).
[68] 1 Samuel 17:26 (NET).
[69] Jeremiah 10:10 (KJV).

Esther from the Old Testament is a story of tension and suspense. Will Esther be selected to become queen? Will Haman's anger and hatred for Esther's uncle cause him to eradicate all of Mordecai's people? The only way to stop him is to engage the young, inexperienced Esther against the cunning Haman in a contest of intellect to influence the king.

Esther tells her uncle that she could be ultimately unsuccessful in her attempt. After all, the king hadn't sent for her for thirty days, and she would be risking her life by coming uninvited into the king's presence unless he extended his golden scepter to her. Mordecai answered her, not with soothing half-truths or comforting lies, but with the cold, hard truth: "Don't imagine that because you are part of the king's household you will be the one Jew who will escape. If you keep quiet at this time, liberation and protection for the Jews will appear from another source, while you and your father's household perish. It may very well be that you have achieved royal status for such a time as this." [70]

As the story goes, the king held out his scepter to Esther, who petitioned him on her people's behalf. Haman was hanged on the very gallows that he built for Mordecai, and the Jews received royal permission to stand against their enemies.

Mordecai's phrase, "for such a time as this," is intriguing. What kind of time is our time? It is definitely a time of challenges. Christians are being murdered and beheaded in places around the entire world. In our homes, we are fighting the influences of drugs and disease, gangs and greed, storms, violence, pollution, and a myriad of other trials and adversity. We certainly live in fearful times.

Esther may have felt secure in the king's household. Still, Mordecai pointed out that the proclamation of destruction would not stop at the palace gates. Perhaps she could have denied her beliefs in an attempt to escape, but escape and denial are responses to fear, not faith.

---

[70] Esther 4:14 (NET).

Esther chose instead to respond with faith. She fasted for three days to spiritually prepare to break the kingdom's law and confront the king. She was well aware of the consequences because, as she stated, "If I perish, I perish." [71] She was willing to risk her life for her cause. Her natural choice was not to live or to die; her choice was the kind of life she would live before she died.

We all have the same choice. What cause will we commit our energy to? Will we choose to live with faith, even in formidable times?

Maxwell Anderson eloquently expresses the choice in his play, *Joan of Lorraine.* As Joan of Arc awaits execution, she addresses her accusers with unassuming simplicity: "Every man gives his life for what he believes. Every woman gives her life for what she believes. Sometimes people believe in little or nothing, nevertheless they give up their lives to that little or nothing. One life is all we have, and we live it as we believe in living it, and then it's gone. But to surrender what you are, and

---

[71] Esther 4:16 (NET).

live without belief—that is more terrible than dying—more terrible than dying young." [72]

We also live in troubling times. Our strength, shield, and defense must be in our witness of Christ. We must develop an energized heart to sustain the internal strength to face the challenges of our day with faith and courage instead of fear and faltering. We need to give our hearts over to Jesus so that he becomes the light of our lives and the touchstone by which we measure every action, every word, and every thought. Only Jesus Christ is uniquely qualified to provide the hope, confidence, and strength to overcome the world and rise above our human failings.

Many of us may not even think about our witness and testimony of Jesus. We may have faith in what our parents taught us. Or we could rely on the strength and conviction of a spouse. Some of us might only have faith in the teachings of a local pastor or the church we belong to but have neglected to build our faith in Christ. Under normal circumstances, these are all good, loving, and worthy voices to rely

---

[72] Anderson, Maxwell, *Joan of Lorraine: A Play in Two Acts* (Washington, D.C.: Anderson House, 1947), 127.

on. Unfortunately, not all fathers are faithful, not all spouses are supportive, and not all churches nurture our individual spiritual needs.

If we ultimately place our faith in fleeting figures and impermanent places, we risk losing the sustainable spirituality that will provide strength and energy to our souls. We need to stay connected to the power of the Son. We need to listen to his voice—to seek it, to listen carefully to distinguish it from all other voices and to pay close attention to its message.

If we explore the Word of God, converse intimately with our God through personal prayer, constantly asking, "What would Jesus say or do in my situation?" then, when a faith-based decision needs to be made, we will know the proper principle to follow and will not be swayed by the loud, competing worldly voices of the faithless fanatics that surround us.

Mother Teresa is an excellent example of a woman with an energized heart. In Bangalore, she was once criticized for "spoiling" people experiencing poverty because she generously dispensed food and goods to them. Mother Teresa persuasively responded, "If I spoil the poor, you and the other sisters spoil the rich in your select schools. And Almighty God is the first to spoil us. Does he not give freely to all of us? Then why should I not imitate my God and give freely to the poor what I have received freely?"[73]

Mother Teresa's clever comeback powerfully and proficiently presented her accusers with a principle of Christianity they both believed in. Mother Teresa's words persuasively reminded them to listen to their own Christian hearts and ask themselves, "What would Jesus have done?"

We live in fearsome times. We need to confront the challenges of our days with the sustained strength of an energized heart. We need to cultivate such a close relationship with Christ and recognize his voice from among all the other voices that clamor around us. Then, we can act with the integrity of an energized Christian.

---

[73] Jose Luis Gonzalez-Galado and Janet N. Playfoot, *My Life for the Poor: Mother Teresa of Calcutta* (San Francisco: Harper & Row, Publishers, 1985), 31.

During the Revolutionary War, darkness fell at noon on May 19, 1780. When the sun peaked, an atmospheric marvel brought the day to an early and unexpected close. People panicked, suspecting that the end of the world had come. [74]

At Hartford, Connecticut, the State Legislature was in session. The Lower House meeting came to a halt in astonishment and wonder. A motion of adjournment was made in the State Senate as legislators prepared to meet the Day of Judgment. But Abraham Davenport, a friend and advisor to George Washington, opposed the motion.

He stood and courteously addressed his legislative associates: "I am against this

---

[74] New England's "Dark Day" occurred on May 19, 1780, when an unusual darkening of the sky was seen during the daytime in New England and parts of Canada. The primary cause of the event is believed to have been a combination of smoke from forest fires, a thick fog, and heavy cloud cover. The day became so dark that candles were necessary to be able to see at noon. This dark cover did not disperse until the following night. For several days before the dark day, the sun appeared red and the sky appeared yellow. Soot collected in rivers and water, suggesting the presence of smoke. Also, when the night actually did come, the moon also appeared red. A New England rain that same morning indicated that cloud cover was present. The most likely cause of the darkness was smoke from a massive forest fire. Researchers examining tree scar damage in what is now Algonquin Provincial Park in Ontario, Canada attribute the dark day to a large fire in that area.

adjournment. The Day of Judgment is either approaching or it is not. If it is not, there is no cause for adjournment. If it is, I choose to be found doing my duty. I wish, therefore, that candles may be brought." [75]

We each face this same choice every day of our existence. We can be found in panic and dismay, or we can be found doing our Christian duty, even in the darkest times, with the light of Christ shining as our candle while we work.

An Energized Religion

The word "religion" has recently taken on a somewhat negative connotation. We hear people proclaim that they see themselves as spiritual but not religious. Perhaps they see religion as being part of a human organization or corporation. In contrast, they see spirituality more as an innate connection with God.

The Bible is the most significant religious text of all time, yet the word "religion" appears only three times in this voluminous manuscript. Paul first uses the word in his

---

[75] Thomas, Lowell, *The Day the Sun Went Out,* in A New Treasury of Words to Live by, edited by William Nichols (New York: Simon and Schuster, 1957), 59-60.

defense before King Agrippa: "According to the strictest party of our religion, I lived as a Pharisee." [76] Of the three sects of the Jews, Pharisees, Sadducees, and Essenes, Paul was a Pharisee, the strictest of the three in ritualistic religious performances.

The word religion appears a second time in Paul's letter to the Galatians. Paul wrote, "You have heard of my way of living in time past in the Jews' religion, how that beyond measure I persecuted the assembly of God, and ravaged it." [77] Most of us are familiar with Paul's persecution of those who professed to be Christians. Paul explains that he had practiced the religion of his fathers—a Hebrew heritage of resolute rules, staunch laws, and tenacious traditions. These pitiless practices caused him to harass the followers of Christ harshly. In both cases, Paul uses the word religion to refer to the rules of practice rather than the doctrines or beliefs.

The final use of the word religion is made by James, who wrote to the twelve tribes. In his letter, James writes, "If someone thinks

---

[76] Acts 26:5 (NET).
[77] Galatians 1:13 (WEB).

he is religious yet does not bridle his tongue, and so deceives his heart, his religion is futile." [78] James uses the term religion similarly to Paul, as something ceremonial or ritualistic. If we are ritualistic in our behavior, he suggests, but don't watch what we say, then our rituals are meaningless. Rituals, by themselves, are powerless. It is our devotion to God that energizes our religious practices.

James emphatically explains what he considers "Pure and undefiled religion before God the Father is this: to care for orphans and widows in their misfortune and to keep oneself unstained by the world." [79] His words are simple and unpretentious, yet their meaning is profound.

To "care for orphans and widows" reminds us to be compassionate to our fellowmen. Just as Jesus frequently taught that we should love our neighbor as ourselves,[80] James uses the fatherless and widows as examples for expressing compassionate service

---

[78] James 1:26 (NET).
[79] James 1:27 (NET).
[80] Matthew 22:39 (NET).

to others and a genuine and energetic devotion to God.

The second half of James' definition of pure religion is to keep ourselves "unstained by the world." Being unstained by the world means being free from the pollution of sin. Paul's writing to the Romans emphasizes the same practice: "Do not be conformed to this present world, but be transformed by the renewing of your mind, so that you may test and approve what is the will of God – what is good and well-pleasing and perfect." [81]

James portrays a pure religion that is a powerful devotion to God, energized by love and compassion for others and strengthened by freedom from sin. In other words, energized religion requires us to refrain from doing wrong while purposefully and persistently performing acts of kindness and assisting others. Matthew said, "Just as you did it for one of the least of these brothers or sisters of mine, you did it for me." [82] Our energized religion should portray the same attributes of service to God and humanity.

---

[81] Romans 12:2.
[82] Matthew 25:40 (NET).

We must not believe that we are not innately religious. Spiritual sustainability will require that we practice an energetic and pure religion in both appearance and in actuality. Our love of purity, decency, honesty, compassion, and kindness is the undeniable confirmation of our innate spirituality. We can encourage its growth and development through devotion to God, demonstrated by love and compassion for others, coupled with unworldliness. Performing kindnesses for others and avoiding unrighteous influences will do more to sustain our spirituality than any ritualistic performance devoid of sincere devotion.

CHAPTER SEVEN

THREE PILLARS OF SPIRITUAL SUSTAINABILITY

The term 'sustainability' originates from the Latin word *sustinere*, which means to hold up. Sustain can mean maintain, support, or endure. Since the early 1980s, the expression 'sustainability' has conveyed a sense of human sustainability on planet earth. The result has been a widely quoted definition of sustainability as "sustainable development that meets the needs of the present without compromising the ability of future generations to meet their own needs."[83]

---

[83] The Brundtland Commission of the United Nations on March 20, 1987.

In 2005, the World Summit on Social Development identified three sustainable development objectives. These objectives, known as the three pillars of sustainability, include economic development, social development, and environmental protection. They are mutually reinforcing and serve as a common ground for numerous sustainability standards.

The term 'sustainable spirituality' may sound simple and vague, but it represents a profound shift in our understanding of spirituality. It's not just about personal growth but also about how our spiritual practices can contribute to the well-being of the planet and future generations. It's a call to action, a task in progress, or a 'journey,' and, therefore, a process.

Sustainability implies responsible and proactive decision-making coupled with innovation that minimizes negative impact while maintaining a balance between ecological resilience, economic prosperity, political justice, and cultural vibrancy to ensure a desirable planet for all species now and in the future.

The development of sustainable spirituality also requires responsible and proactive progress toward specific objectives. The three sustainable spirituality objectives include prayer, study, and service. They are the common ground for developing spiritual strength and are also mutually reinforcing.

Prayer is not just a ritual but a powerful tool that allows individuals to connect with God and foster inner peace. It enables them to reflect on their intentions and actions, serving as a foundation for mindfulness. Through prayer, practitioners can cultivate gratitude and compassion as they explore their place in the world, leading to a sense of calm and centeredness.

Study engages individuals in deepening their understanding of Biblical texts, philosophies, and teachings. This intellectual exploration enriches one's spirituality by offering insights into moral principles, ethics, and our connectedness to God. Through study, individuals can challenge preconceptions and grow in wisdom.

Service is not just about giving back to the community; it is a way to embody the values learned through prayer and study. By actively participating in acts of kindness and support for others, individuals reinforce their commitment to sustainability. Service fosters relationships built on empathy, demonstrating how our lives are intertwined with those around us, making us feel more engaged and connected.

Used together—prayer nurtures introspection; study enriches knowledge; service embodies action—the three objectives create a holistic approach to sustainable spirituality that encourages personal growth while contributing positively to society at large. As adherents embrace these practices, they cultivate resilience against challenges while seeking harmony within themselves and with the planet.

Developing sustainable spirituality is accomplished only through deliberate effort and a specific call to action. Developing sustainable spirituality and attuning ourselves to the greatest influences of heaven is unquestionably a challenging process. It takes time and often involves an exerted effort. It does not happen by chance but is accomplished through deliberate determination.

Paul often used examples and expressions from athletic contests to convey his argument about spiritual growth. He proposed that a Christian successfully obeying God's commandments is comparable to an athlete winning a contest. The similarities between the two are training, exertion, obeying rules, personal discipline, and the desire to win.

In writing to the Corinthians, Paul says, "Don't you know that those who run in a race all run, but one receives the prize? Run like that, that you may win. Every man who strives in the games exercises self-control in all things. Now they do it to receive a corruptible crown, but we an incorruptible. I therefore run like that, as not uncertainly." [84]

He comparably wrote to his friend, Timothy, "I have competed well; I have finished the race; I have kept the faith! Finally the crown of righteousness is reserved for me. The Lord, the righteous Judge, will award it to me in that day – and not to me only, but also

---

[84] 1 Corinthians 9:24-26 (WEB).

to all who have set their affection on his appearing." [85]

In Paul's day, an athletic contest was sometimes a hand-to-hand confrontation to the death. Considering this extreme nature of the competition, Paul wrote,

"Clothe yourself with the full armor of God so that you may be able to stand against the schemes of the devil. For our struggle is not against flesh and blood but against the rulers, against the powers, against the world rulers of this darkness, against the spiritual forces of evil in high places.

"Clothe yourself with the full armor of God so that you may be able to stand against the schemes of the devil. For our struggle is not against flesh and blood but against the rulers, against the powers, against the world rulers of this darkness, against the spiritual forces of evil in high places.

"For this reason take up the full armor of God so that you may be able to stand your

---

[85] 2 Timothy 4:7, 8 (NET).

ground on the evil day, and having done everything, to stand.

"Stand firm therefore, by fastening the belt of truth around your waist, by putting on the breastplate of righteousness,

"By fitting your feet with the preparation that comes from the good news of peace,

"And in all of this, by taking up the shield of faith with which you can extinguish all the flaming arrows of the evil one.

"And take the helmet of salvation and the sword of the Spirit, which is the word of God.

"With every prayer and petition, pray at all times in the Spirit, and to this end be alert, with all perseverance and requests for all the saints." [86]

God created us with magnificent minds capable of learning and spiritual strength, which may be amplified in proportion to our obedience to God. The closer we are to God, the nearer God is to us. Our convictions can

---

[86] Ephesians 6:11-18 (NET).

be more precise, life's pleasures can be more significant, and we can lose all desire to sin.

Part of the struggle as we strive to acquire sustainable spirituality is the feeling that it is too far out of reach. We may feel we fall too short of the prize, but we can capitalize on our strengths. Starting right where we are today, we can seek the happiness that is found in pursuing the spiritual things of God.

The place to begin is here. The time to start is now. The effort can be simply one step at a time. A simple prayer silently spoken from the heart, a page of scripture studied and applied to our personal circumstances, a small act of kindness performed for someone in need will move us toward our spiritual objective. God will lead us along, and we will, through persistent progress, approach the glorious prize.

Every person on earth can make spiritual progress. The gospel of Jesus Christ is more than a robust code of ethics, more than an ideal social order, more than a program of positive thinking or self-improvement. It is a divine plan for spiritual growth and sustainability. It is the saving power of the Lord

Jesus Christ. With faith in Christ, we can move a step at a time, improving as we go, asking for strength, and refining our attitudes and ambitions until we find ourselves securely in the fold of the Good Shepherd.

Undoubtedly, it will require discipline, training, exertion, and strength. But as the Apostle Paul said, "I can do all things through Christ who strengthens me." [87]

At a decisive moment in the battle of Waterloo, a concerned courier rode up to the Duke of Wellington to inform him that, unless they retreated immediately, they would fall before the impending assault of the French army. The Duke replied, "Stand firm!"

"But we shall perish," argued the officer.

"Stand firm!" the Duke again responded.

"You'll find us there!" replied the courier, and he galloped away.

The British were victorious that day due to the Duke's determination and the

---

loyalty of his soldiers. [88] Another battle with even bleaker consequences is being fought today. It is the battle for the souls of humanity. The outcome similarly hinges on the steadiness of the soldiers. The call of the Commander is still, "Stand firm!"

We must stand firm and remain faithful to the kingdom of God as we live our Christian beliefs in the quiet commonplace of our daily lives. We can do so as we learn to rely on the three pillars of sustainable spirituality.

---

[88] Baxendale, Walter, ed., *Dictionary of Anecdote, Incident, Illustrative Fact* [New York, 1889], 225.

CHAPTER EIGHT

THE PILLAR OF PERSONAL PRAYER

The moral pollution index in our society is rising. The devil is on the loose. Without the sustaining infusion of spiritual power through communion with God, Christians are no stronger than anyone else. We cannot resist the constant pull of immorality. We cannot elude the desensitization from the daily doses of violence and cruelty on our own. We are all vulnerable to satanic influences and too susceptible to confront the enemy alone.

But we can refine and purify our lives through the regular practice of prayer. We can call on God when we are overjoyed or overwhelmed. We can voice our souls' deepest desires when we have been blessed or when we have been humbled to the dust. We can stand confidently in his mighty cause, knowing that God is with us no matter the enormity of the enemy's ranks.

As Christians, our prayer life—how often we pray, how earnestly we pray, and how trustingly we pray—is an unerring measure of our sustainable spirituality. Sustainable spirituality is a consistent and enduring connection with God that is not easily disrupted. Prayer keeps us from sinning; sinning keeps us from prayer. We cannot climb the mountain of spirituality without raising our hearts and voices in fervent prayer to God.

As we become more prayerful, we develop a greater sustainable faith in God, trusting and relying on spiritual powers much more significant than our mortal power. Prayer builds and sustains spiritual strength beyond our limited abilities by providing us access to an all-powerful God. We can do plenty on our own, but some things can only be accomplished with divine assistance.

The powerful gift of prayer permits us to cultivate a close relationship with God and Christ. Through prayer, we convey our deepest needs, our earnest personal feelings, and our heartfelt desires to God and then ask sincerely for his help.

Our lives are largely the product of the friendships we foster. The more we develop a close association with God, the greater our characteristics will become. We will develop the capacity to rise above the petty and insignificant trivialities of our mortal sins and fears. Just as a continual association with degrading influences will adversely affect us, a persistent connection with God will elevate and improve us.

By engaging our hearts and minds in sincere prayer, God, through his Holy Spirit, will infuse our souls with purpose and a greater personal power and influence. As we gain greater strength from an omnipotent Being, our spirits will become instilled with a sustainable spiritual energy.

Some prayers are simple, joyful expressions of gratitude. Some are deep pleadings for our heavy sorrows to be lifted.

And some prayers are impassioned struggles for a greater spiritual connection with God. Some prayers pour freely from our hearts, while others require strenuous and disciplined effort. Jacob wrestled with an angel throughout the night until he obtained his desired blessing from God. [89]

Jesus understood this powerful principle of prayer as he poured his heart out to his Father on the Mount of Olives. "And in his anguish," Luke tells us, "he prayed more earnestly." [90] What a marvelous and noteworthy statement! The Son of God "prayed more earnestly."

Jesus did all things correctly. His every word was true, and his every deed was proper. He was the only perfect being to walk the dusty paths of planet Earth. And yet, Jesus Christ, the Son of God, "prayed more earnestly." His example shows us that not all prayers are alike. Greater need requires more serious and faith-filled persuading before the throne of God.

Of course, not all prayers will require such a consorted effort on our part, but some

---

89 See Genesis 32:24-32.
90 Luke 22:44 (NET).

"thorns in the flesh [91]"—persistent challenges or struggles in our lives—will demand prayers of significant strength and intensity. Just as Jacob did not wrestle with God in every prayer every day, our prayers will not all involve the full, soul-wrenching effort required for specific troublesome times. But if we are willing to invest the time and energy to pray more earnestly, then miracles will begin to take place in our lives.

Our prayers will then become edifying and instructive, and God can show us many essential and pertinent things. Paul taught that "the Spirit helps us in our weakness, for we do not know how we should pray, but the Spirit himself intercedes for us with inexpressible groanings." [92]

In other words, when we are attentive, the Spirit of the Lord can help us pray for things we might not have thought of on our own, deeply spiritual things beyond our physical human desires. We can find our words surpassing our thoughts as the Spirit assists us

---

[91] See 2 Corinthians 12:7-10.
[92] Romans 8:26 (NET).

in praying for people, possibilities, and prospects in ways that may astound us.

We could encounter obstacles in developing such a spiritually sustaining communion with God that will inhibit us from enjoying the relationship that we would like to have. When we pray to God, we have no one to impress and no judgment to fear. He knows all things, including the desires of our hearts. Therefore, we should only speak the words that we truly feel.

Our prayers should be plain and simple. We should ask for what we want the same way we would ask an earthly parent, "Hey Dad, can I borrow the car tonight?"

In Shakespeare's play Hamlet, Claudius ceased praying because his heart was not in his prayers. He said,

"My words fly up, my thoughts remain below;

Words without thoughts never to heaven go." [93]

---

[93] Shakespeare, William, *Hamlet*, Act 3, Scene 3.

Physical distractions and concerns can be a hindrance to effective prayer. It can be helpful if we slow down, stop what we're doing, and sit quietly before we approach God. Listening to inspiring music or reading a few verses of the Bible can help us contemplate and reflect before prayer.

Duplicity is another roadblock to an effective prayer. We can't expect to pray effectively at night if we are sinful throughout the day. Henry Ward Beecher said, "It is not well for a man to pray cream and live skim milk." Today, we see a greater tendency for people to pray skim milk and not even live that. The more faithful we are in keeping God's commandments and putting him first, the wider he opens the doors of communication with us.

Another area for improvement is praying with little thought, reflection, or devotion. When our prayers are only a spasmodic cry for help in a crisis, our petitions become entirely selfish. God is not a repairman we call on only in emergencies. We should remember to pray in the good and bad times, not only when all other support has failed and we feel desperate. Remember, if you only pray when you're in trouble, you're in trouble!

Answers to Prayers

Understand that God answers prayers. We haven't developed a sustainable level of faith and spirituality until we understand that we can pray, listen, and know when our prayers are answered. We can get close to God. He isn't an absentee parent. He will be as close to us as we allow him to be.

Each of us will experience a time when we pray but do not seem to receive the answer we seek. God is willing to give and will give all that he sees is good for us, even when he doesn't give us all we ask for. We should recognize and follow the example Jesus set when we petition God and say, "Not my will but yours be done." [94] And then remember, sometimes the answer is no.

Receiving answers to our prayers requires we make a sincere effort. Our intention should be honest, the desire of our hearts should be truthful, and we should have

---

[94] Luke 22:42 (NET).

enough faith in Christ to request and receive what we seek.

Receiving answers is facilitated when we have a deep feeling of spiritual need. It is more than just saying words and receiving answers. Through a sense of humility and dependence on God, we can have answers to our prayers.

Answers will come to the extent that we diligently follow God's law. In humility, we should ask, as Paul did, "Lord, what wilt thou have me to do?" [95] With undaunted courage, we should say, as Samuel did, "Speak, Lord, for your servant is listening." [96] Then, when God tells you what to do, you had better have the faith to do it or not ask again.

Sustainable spirituality comes from prayer. Prayer is our passport to spiritual power. Prayer doesn't ever promise us freedom from adversity and affliction. Instead, it offers us a channel of communication to seek divine help and spiritual guidance.

---

[95] Acts 9:6 (KJV).
[96] 1 Samuel 3:9 (NET).

CHAPTER NINE

THE PILLAR OF PERSONAL STUDY

The word of God is a powerful instrument of rebirth, transforming us into new creatures in Christ. As he journeyed to Damascus, Stephen's testimony undoubtedly stirred the heart of Saul of Tarsus, demonstrating the profound transformative power of the word of God. [97]

Paul later wrote about the importance of personal human testimony:

"For everyone who calls on the name of the Lord shall be saved.

---

[97] See Acts 7; 9.

"How are they to call on one they have not believed in? And how are they to believe in one they have not heard of? And how are they to hear without someone preaching to them?

"And how are they to preach unless they are sent? As it is written, 'How timely is the arrival of those who proclaim the good news.'

"…Consequently faith comes from what is heard, and what is heard comes through the preached word of Christ." [98]

The Bible is a powerful witness for Jesus Christ and his gospel. In addition, it is essential to consider what we can learn from other people's experiences in it. A review of the historical events in the Bible allows us to see a reflection of our own lives. We can compare circumstances and conditions in our time with those in relevant segments of Biblical history and predict the consequences of our own human behavior with a sense of accuracy. We can learn how to warrant God's blessings and avoid the catastrophes that frequently followed the people in Biblical times.

---

[98] Romans 10:13-15, 17 (NET).

Human writing may be witty and sometimes even wise, but the word of God touches the core of what matters most and goes straight to the heart of life's most critical issues. There is great virtue and great power in the word of God. People have completely turned their lives around and become converted simply by reading the pure witness of the word.

The power of the Bible is not in its sophistication nor in its appeal to the wise. Its sustaining power emanates from God to its readers. "Our gospel did not come to you merely in words, but in power and in the Holy Spirit and with deep conviction." [99] It transcends the interests of style and delivers substance instead.

Paul told the Corinthians, "I did not come with superior eloquence or wisdom as I proclaimed the testimony of God. For I decided to be concerned about nothing among you except Jesus Christ, and him crucified. And I was with you in weakness and in fear and in much trembling. My conversation and my preaching were not with persuasive words of

---

[99] 1 Thessalonians 1:5 (NET).

wisdom, but with a demonstration of the Spirit and with power, so that your faith would not be based on human wisdom but on the power of God." [100]

The word of God by itself is so powerful that gospel teachers do not need to shoulder the burden of converting their listeners. With all of the reading, studying, preparing, praying, organizing, and presenting a minister or a teacher may do, the spiritual lesson is presented by the Spirit. He is the true teacher and the sole converter, conveying the word of truth into our hearts and minds. This is how the Spirit sustains our faith and strengthens our testimony—through the power and conviction of the word of God.

We all respond differently to the word of truth, and sometimes, we are unaware of the effect of our reading or the good that it does. Stephen [101] succumbed to a cruel death at the hands of wicked men. (I don't imagine that it is an easy thing to die for our convictions, but death must be much sweeter for those who die bearing fervent witness of Christ.) And so

---

[100] 1 Corinthians 2:1-5 (NET).
[101] See Acts 7.

Stephen was put to death. But the testament lived on. Faith came to Paul, who heard the word of God preached by a faithful testator for Christ.

When we immerse ourselves in the Bible regularly and consistently, our level of sustainable spirituality increases significantly. Our testimony of the truth will grow, and our commitment to the cause of Christ will be strengthened.

Increased integrity, the power to resist temptation, and daily guidance and direction are a few of the promises God offers us when we feast on his word. If God tells us that these things will come through his word, then those blessings will be ours. Blessings are found in the Holy Scriptures. By accepting the word of God, we can navigate through the mists of darkness and come to Christ.

Profiting from Bible Study

The Bible offers us fascinating vicarious experiences. Of the billions who live on earth, no one can walk with God like Adam did. We don't have the privilege and opportunity to speak with God like Moses did.

But the Bible is available to nearly every soul; through it, we can become personally acquainted with God and his Son Jesus Christ.

The Bible vividly portrays humanity's weaknesses, strengths, and subsequent rewards and punishments. It clarifies the good and illuminates the evil. We can quickly learn life's lessons when we see the good and poor choices of others in the past. The faithfulness of God's followers under stress, temptation, and persecution can strengthen and sustain our resolve.

Studying Job, we learn to keep faith through the greatest of adversities. Reading how Joseph, engulfed in the luxuries of Egypt and tempted by Potiphar's wife, resisted all the powers of darkness, should certainly sustain us against similar sin.

Examining Peter's growth as the catalyst of the Good News, which advances him from an uncultured and unlearned fisherman into a great organizer, theologian, and teacher, will sustain our courage and conviction that nothing but ourselves can stop our spiritual progress.

Witnessing Paul's forbearance and fortitude in giving his life to Christ adds courage when we feel injured and tried. Paul was beaten and imprisoned, stoned and robbed, shipwrecked, and nearly drowned. He was the victim of false friends and underhanded associates. At times, starving, choking, freezing, and poorly clothed, Paul remained consistent in his service. He never faltered after his witness came to him.

Watching Saul progress from a donkey tender to the king of Israel and then seeing his arrogance and pride drive him down from his throne to the tent of Endor's witch-like a man gone mad; to see him defeated in battle, his decapitated head displayed for his enemies to spit at will undoubtedly teach us a valuable lesson on pride and arrogance.

The Bible is straightforward in its approach. It is tough on the rebellious and wicked but soothing and healing to the repentant sinner.

Jesus advised us to "study the scriptures thoroughly because you think in them you possess eternal life." [102] In Jesus' life, we discover the valuable qualities of goodness, strength, self-control, and godliness. By studying this great Book, we can capture some of those qualities for ourselves. These vital scriptures are the essence of courage, faith, and fortitude. They portray perseverance, great sacrifice, and super-human accomplishments. They contain stories of intrigue, vengeance, adversity, war, murder, idolatry, miracles, revelations, and prophecy. The Bible is life at its best and at its worst. It carries us through colossal crises and then engulfs us in God's great love.

We shouldn't overestimate our Biblical education. Many of us have a few favorite verses of scripture at our somewhat immediate mental disposal, drifting aimlessly somewhere in our minds. This creates the illusion that we know and understand much of the Bible. At some point in our lives, we really need to uncover more of these hidden truths for ourselves. If we want to become spiritually sustainable, we need to make the lessons of the

---

[102] John 5:39 (NET).

Bible a regular and well-known part of our lives.

If we enthusiastically pursue a study of the Bible with a conscientious and persistent effort, we will find answers to our problems and peace in our hearts. We will feel the Holy Spirit expanding our awareness with new and greater insights. The doctrines of Christ will become more meaningful and certain, and we will gain greater wisdom to direct and determine the course of our lives. We will also become a light and a strength to non-believers.

Access to the Bible requires responsibility for its teachings. God isn't kidding when he tells us, "to whoever much is given, of him will much be required." [103] We don't receive eternal life without becoming "doers of the word," [104] fearless in obeying God's law. We can't become "doers" without first being "hearers." God's word has always been given to those with "eyes to see" and "ears to hear." As "hearers," we can't simply wait for random pieces of information to find

---

[103] Luke 12:48 (NET).
[104] James 1:22 (NET).

their way into our minds; we need to seek and study.

God's voice is clear and unmistakable. If you haven't already done so, I ask you to begin to study the scriptures earnestly. Neglecting Bible study will rob us of the strength to sustain our spirituality.

CHAPTER TEN

THE PILLAR OF SERVICE TO OTHERS

When the Apostle Paul declared that "love is patient and kind," [105] he wasn't just talking about being nice to one another and smiling at each other all day long. He was revealing to us the core and heart of Christian living. Kindness without love is not kindness at all. It's patronage, condescension, and snobbery. It's merely a transactional gesture, lacking the depth and warmth that love brings. True kindness flows from a place of genuine care and compassion, where we seek to understand others' feelings and experiences.

---

[105] 1 Corinthians 13:4 (NET).

Love adds purpose to our actions; it transforms simple acts into meaningful connections. When kindness is infused with love, it becomes an expression of empathy, fostering relationships built on trust and respect. In this way, we create a ripple effect — inspiring others to act kindly in return, deepening our bonds, and nurturing a more compassionate world. Without love as its foundation, kindness is empty and arrogant; it's through loving intentions that our acts resonate profoundly in the hearts of those around us. Anyone who has received this type of "kindness" knows they are better off without it. But when reinforced with love, kind deeds create refreshing connections and build friendly bonds.

Mother Teresa says, "it is not very often things [the poor] need. What they need much more is what we offer them. In these twenty years of work amongst the people, I have come more and more to realize that it is being unwanted that is the worst disease that any human being can ever experience. Nowadays we have found medicine for leprosy and lepers can be cured. There's medicine for TB and consumptives can be cured. For all kinds of diseases there are medicines and cures. But for being unwanted, except there are willing hands to serve and there's a loving heart to love, I don't think this terrible disease can ever be cured." [106]

Simple human kindness from the heart is the cure. Kindness is not complicated. It's little things done consistently with a cumulative impact. It's the simple acts—a smile, a compliment, holding the door open for someone, or helping without expecting anything in return. These small gestures might seem insignificant on their own, but when they accumulate over time and are woven into our daily lives, they create a ripple effect of positivity.

Imagine how much brighter someone's day can become with just a few words of encouragement or appreciation. Kindness fosters connections and builds bridges between people. It allows us to understand one another better and nurtures an environment where empathy thrives.

---

[106] Quoted in Malcolm Muggeridge, *Something Beautiful for God: Mother Teresa of Calcutta* (New York: Walker and Company/Phoenix Press, 1971, large print edition 1984), 96.

Furthermore, kindness has a way of coming back around. When we choose to be kind to others, it often inspires them to pay it forward, creating a chain reaction that spreads far beyond what we can see at the moment. The world becomes just a bit lighter as more individuals are touched by goodwill.

Often, we feel we don't have the time or the resources to make any real and significant difference in someone else's life. But, no matter how small or seemingly insignificant the effort, we can all do what we can. In a compilation of letters to God, a young girl wrote, "Dear God, I am sending you a penny to give to a kid poorer than me. Love, Donna." [107] Well, a penny certainly isn't very much. Most of us wouldn't even stoop to pick one up off the sidewalk. But this simple act of generosity reveals the kindness of this little girl's heart. There's nothing insignificant about that!

I once read a story about a man on a bus who was allowed to perform a kind service to a woman in need. The woman slumped in

---

[107] Marshall, Eric and Hample, Stuart, comps. *Children's Letters to God,* enl. ed. (New York: Pocket Books, 1975).

her seat near the front of the bus. She was visibly weary and overwhelmed. Her unkempt hair lay matted against her dirty face. It was the middle of winter, but this poor woman wore a flimsy cotton dress and a blanket with torn-out arm holes. It is evident that she was in desperate hardship.

The man on the bus wanted to help her and pondered what he could do. Maybe he could direct her to a shelter, and they could help her. Her plight and problems appeared too overwhelmingly complex for this one man to handle. As he thought of, and subsequently dismissed, possible solutions to the poor woman's predicament, the bus stopped.

Another young man, in neat but inexpensive attire, stood up to exit the bus. It wasn't until the bus had started on its way again that the first man noticed what this young man had done. He had slipped off his black knit gloves and laid them on the poor woman's lap. [108]

That young man couldn't solve all the poor woman's worries and troubles, nor did he

---

[108] Sisley, Jr., John H., untitled anecdote *in The Prince of Peace Is Born* (pamphlet) (Carmel, NY: Guideposts Associates, 1991).

try, but he saw her cold, red hands and knew he could do something about them. And he did.

Kindness is no more complicated than that; we can all do similar kind deeds for one another daily. Small acts of kindness ripple like water in a pond, except, in the case of kindness, the ripples grow stronger as they go.

Kindness is self-sustaining, and a Christian heart is impulsively kind. Kindness creates a confident and caring association with another human being, even with a stranger we may never see again. It is incredible how quickly Christ's love can fill our hearts from even a tiny act of kindness. It is deeply empowering! Kindness really is its own reward.

When the Dalai Lama was asked to describe the Tibetan religion, he said, "My religion is very simple. My religion is kindness." [109] But kindness is also the heart of the Christian religion.

Christian kindness comes from the heart. It is kindness for kindness' sake alone,

---

[109] Dalai Lama, as quoted in Editors of Canari Press, *Random Acts of Kindness* (Berkeley, CA: Conari Press, 1993), 20.

not because we're expecting some great payoff or because we want others to notice how righteous and good we are. Christians should never expect any external reward.

Wilma Hepker studied burnout in community volunteers and made this powerful observation: "If we're willing to help only perfect people, we might as well shut down everything right now because there aren't any perfect people out there to help.

"No, if you're going to survive volunteering, you can't do so because you think the people you're helping deserve it. You can't help people because they'll thank you. You have to help them because Christ loves them and He's loving them through you. You volunteer because in doing so, you represent Christ to them in the here and now—even if they don't see Him in you." [110]

We've all experienced kindness and unkindness; consequently, we can easily recognize how it feels when someone is kind to us. Hopefully, we also recognize the subtle feeling in our hearts when we are kind to

---

[110] Hepker, Wilma, *"Survival Tactics for Volunteers"* Signs of the Times, October 1993, 13.

someone else. It's a feeling that is hard to describe but easy to identify. Very little in this life is as comforting during heartache as receiving the kindness of others—unless, of course, it's being able to perform some random kindness ourselves. We've all heard that, "If you want to feel better yourself, do something for someone else." This is literally true.

Christian kindness is a genuine expression of love and compassion that reflects the teachings of Jesus Christ. This kindness encourages us to treat others with respect, empathy, and understanding, regardless of their circumstances or beliefs.

When we embody Christian kindness, we serve as instruments of grace in our communities. We approach those suffering or marginalized with open arms and listening ears, recognizing that everyone deserves dignity and support. It's about looking beyond ourselves and finding ways to uplift others—sharing our resources, time, and attention.

Christian kindness compels us to forgive those who have wronged us. It invites us to let go of grudges and extend mercy instead, fostering healing for ourselves and those around us. Through acts of service, words of encouragement, or simply offering a smile during difficult times, we can create ripples of positivity that resonate far beyond our immediate interactions.

In essence, Christian kindness is an active choice—a commitment to living out our faith through deeds big and small. By allowing this virtue to guide our daily actions, we build a more loving world where hope thrives amidst challenges. Exploring opportunities for random acts of kindness becomes integral; even simple gestures like complimenting someone or helping a neighbor can profoundly impact individuals' lives.

We should always offer kindness wherever we can, even when fairness does not require it. We should live with greater attention to the love, hope, and compassion Jesus Christ displayed toward others. We can always treat each other with a little more kindness, courtesy, and greater humility, patience, and forgiveness.

Paul told the Corinthians how they could recognize a true representative of Christ: "By purity, by knowledge, by patience, by benevolence (kindness), by the Holy Spirit, by genuine love." [111] The world today needs more Christ-like love and kindness. It is an invitation that we can all accept. We should never allow any occasion to be kind to pass us by. Kindness has an infinite ability to fill our lives with profound meaning and deep significance.

---

[111] 2 Corinthians 6:6 (NET).

CHAPTER ELEVEN

A FOUNDATION OF CHARITY

Jesus gave us "a new commandment," identifying us as his disciples. He directed us "to love one another.… Everyone will know by this that you are my disciples." [112] The love we carry for the human family is the same love Jesus extends to everyone. It is the loftiest height the human soul can reach and the most profound utterance of the human heart.

It is difficult to assign a specific definition to the English word love. The expression "I love pizza" is very different from

---

[112] John 13:34, 35 (NET).

the expression "I love my spouse" (or at least it should be!), yet we use the same word to express both emotions. Ancient Greeks used four distinct words to define love: Agape, Phileo, Strogene, and Eros. Ancient Greek is the language of the New Testament.

Agape, the highest form of love, is divine in nature. It is love that emanates from God, perfect, pure, and self-sacrificing. The scripture "God is love" [113] refers to agape. The King James Version of the Bible translates the word *agape* as *charity*. [114] a term that transcends mere feelings and emotions.

For our world to remain spiritually sustainable, it needs the pure love of Christ. The standard of charity is the only path to peace for our world. If our hearts are filled with charity, we will be kinder, gentler, and more forgiving. We will be slower to anger and more willing to help. We will extend the hand of friendship and withhold the hand of retribution. We will love one another with genuine compassion, mirroring God's love for

---

[113] 1 John 4:8 (NET).
[114] See 1 Corinthians 13 (KJV).

us, and we will walk the path Jesus walked more resolutely.

We all want a peaceful world with peaceful neighborhoods and families. Securing and sustaining such a tranquil setting involves learning to love each other, our friends, and our enemies. A peaceful world requires the pure love of Christ. It entails loving each other with the same self-sacrificing love that Paul calls agape or charity.

A sure indication of our spiritual sustainability is our increased capability to love. Pure love is centered on God. John wrote, "God is love, and the one who resides in love resides in God, and God resides in him." [115] Pure love can only come from a pure source, and that source is God. God loves purely, absolutely, and perfectly. John understood that we love God because he first loved us. [116]

The most significant indication of God's love is the gift of his Beloved Son. God "so loved the world, that he gave his one and only Son, that whoever believes in him should

---

[115] 1 John 4:16 (NET).
[116] 1 John 4:10, 19 (NET).

not perish, but have eternal life." [117] Anyone who has had the burden of sin removed, the heaviness of guilt lifted. The suffering of resentment, anger, or agony relieved by the healing hand of Christ knows the purifying, cleansing feeling of the pure love of Christ.

Our love for God will grow as we acknowledge his goodness, gain greater awareness of his involvement in our lives, and recognize his influence in everything honorable, good, and worthy in our individual circumstances and situations. All our personal desires, whether physical or spiritual, should be set in the love of God.

Jesus acknowledged the destitute and the deprived, infants and widows, farmers and fishermen, shepherds and goat herders. He recognized strangers and foreigners, the prominent wealthy and powerful politicians, and even the unfavorable Pharisees and scribes.

He cared for the poor, the hungry, and the sick. He blessed the disabled, the blind, and the deaf. He forgave people burdened with sin.

---

[117] John 3:16 (WEB).

He taught love, which was demonstrated by his unselfish service to others. No one was ever denied Christ's love.

Sustainable spirituality requires us to purify our inner feelings, change our hearts, and make our outward actions and appearance conform to what we say, believe, and feel inside. It requires us to become true disciples of Christ.

In the scope of our Christian lives and a world filled with so much need and sorrow, we all have ample opportunity to hear someday Christ say to us, "For I was hungry and you gave me food, I was thirsty and you gave me something to drink, I was a stranger, and you invited me in, I was naked and you gave me clothing, I was sick and you took care of me, I was in prison and you visited me."

At that moment, we may wonder when we did these kindnesses for our Lord. We may turn to him confused and ask, "Lord, when did we see you hungry and feed you, or thirsty and give you something to drink, or a stranger and invite you in, or naked and clothe you? When did we see you in prison and visit you?"

Then Jesus will answer us, "Just as you did it for one of the least of these brothers or sisters of mine, you did it for me." [118]

Random acts of kindness, good deeds, and works of faith are much more meaningful when substantiated by God's love. As new creatures in Christ, we should serve others with pure and proper intention. Paul explains the spiritual sustainability of this exceptional form of love in his letter to the Corinthians, where he writes, "Love never fails." [119]

Christians ought to love each other. We share similar interests in the things that matter most in this life. Our life's purpose, goals, ambitions, hopes, and dreams center on Jesus Christ. But this exceptional expression of love should not be restricted to just those of similar faith and feelings. We must not remain content in simply loving the Christian family alone. We have an obligation beyond the fold of Christ that reaches the entire world, and we should be anxious to bless all of humanity.

---

[118] Matthew 25:35-40 (NET).
[119] 1 Corinthians 13:8 (WEB).

We should develop a love for all people everywhere. Our hearts should reach out to everyone in the pure love of God.

Four Obstacles to Pure Love

Christian love is so vital to the sustainability of our spiritual selves that Satan works constantly at setting up stumbling blocks and barriers to the practice of this spiritual gift. Things seem to "get in the way" to prevent us from sharing the love of God with others. The following are some of the more common obstacles to pure love:

1. *Egocentricity.* When we become self-absorbed, we cannot feel the pure love of Christ or effectively share it with other people. The love of God is not a love of personal gratification. Pure love pursues the joy and happiness of others. Christ's commission to "love your neighbor as yourself" [120] has little concern with loving ourselves; its interest and focus is in loving others and exemplifying the Golden Rule taught by Jesus in the sermon at Galilee. [121] The irony of the gospel of Jesus

---

[120] Matthew 19:19 (NET).
[121] See Matthew 7:12.

Christ is that only by losing our life can we truly find it. [122]

2. *Deceitfulness.* By opening ourselves to the truth and living in harmony with that truth, we can develop God-like love. In Dostoyevsky's classic work, The Brothers Karamazov, Zossima says to Feodor, "A man who lies to himself and who listens to his own lies gets to a point where he can't "A man who lies to himself and who listens to his own lies gets to a point where he can't distinguish any truth in himself or in those around him, and so loses all respect for himself and for others. Having no respect for anyone, he ceases to love, and to occupy and distract himself without love he becomes a prey to his passions and gives himself up to coarse pleasures…and all this from continual lying to people and to himself." [123]

3. *Sin.* Wickedness weakens love, and lust is a pitiful substitute for pure love. The love God bestows on us is a spiritual gift given because of our faithfulness. Sin naturally

---

[122] See Matthew 16:25.
[123] Dostoyevsky, *The Brothers Karamazov*, p. 47.

prevents us from fully receiving and sharing this gift.

4. *Thoughtlessness.* We offend and alienate the Holy Spirit when we characterize vulgar, cruel, uncaring language and behaviors. Man's inhumanity to man, whether in the form of viciousness and violence or simply sarcasm and insult, will, over time, desensitize us to the tender and sympathetic feelings that foster and encourage pure love.

Active and sincere love based on Jesus of Nazareth's teachings is undoubtedly the world's greatest need. But much of the world today rejects those teachings. Spiritual sustainability requires that sincere Christians proclaim the truth of Christ's teachings and demonstrate to everyone the power and peace of a righteous, gentle life.

Jesus counsels us to "love your enemies, bless them that curse you, do good to them that hate you, and pray for them which despitefully use you, and persecute you." [124] Imagine the change this concept alone could create in our neighborhoods, local

---

[124] Matthew 5:44 (KJV).

communities, and the countries that comprise our great global family.

If loving our enemies seems like an unreasonable and unrealistic challenge, consider instead the dreadful, deadly challenges waged by war, posed by poverty, created by crime, and all the piercing pain caused by these past solutions.

What should we do when someone we love hurts us? How should we react when we are mistreated? What happens within our hearts when we are lied to, treated unkindly, misunderstood, or sinned against?

Should we fight back? Should we counter with an even larger barrage of offenses, insults, and lies? Do we give an eye for an eye and a tooth for a tooth? Such solutions are far from sustainable and, as Tevye from Fiddler on the Roof suggests, will only leave us blind and toothless.

These situations allow us to practice our Christian values and lifestyle. They also provide us with an invaluable opportunity to forgive others their debts as we seek similar forgiveness from our Father. [125]

Jesus' message of love, as one writer so eloquently states, "flowed forth as sweetly and as lavishly to single listeners as to enraptured crowds; and some of its very richest revelations were vouchsafed, neither to rulers nor to multitudes, but to the persecuted outcast of the Jewish synagogue, to the timid inquirer in the lonely midnight, and the frail woman by the noonday well.

"His teachings dealt not so much with ceremony and minutia as with the human soul, and human destiny, and human life filled with faith and hope and charity.

"Springing from the depths of holy emotions, [his teachings] thrilled the being of every listener as with an electric flame.

"In a word, his authority was the authority of God. Christ's voice was pure and pervaded with sympathy. Even the severity of

---

[125] See Matthew 6:12.

his sternest injunctions was expressed with an unutterable love."[126]

God's pure love is the "more excellent way" [127] Paul described that constitutes one of the greatest gifts God has given us. Christians should serve others [128] but service without love is no service at all. Christians should serve others, but service without love is no service at all. Christian love is the noblest form of love. It is a gift of the Spirit that elevates us to increased kindness and compassion for others. We can serve without loving, but we can't genuinely love without serving. If you want to reach out to God, try reaching out to some of his other children here on Earth.

We must develop the sustaining power of Christ-like love before we can render all the Christian service we want and never gain a deep-rooted, permanent, and fully sustainable Christian character. Paul understood this. He cautioned against giving away our possessions to feed the poor if we are missing the Christ-like quality of pure love to back up our

---

[126] Farrar, Frederic W., *The Life of Christ* [Portland, Oregon: Fountain Publications, 1964], 215.
[127] 1 Corinthians 12:31 (NET).
[128] See James 2:8.

intentions. [129] When imbued with pure love, we perform Christian service not because we think it's the right thing to do but because that is simply who we are.

Now that we have discussed the ideal of developing a sustainable God-like love, where do we go from here? We know that our service and deeds should be motivated by pure love, but what do we do if our motives fall short of our knowledge and expectations? We can still try to do what is right, even if our hearts are not fully invested. We can ask God to give substance and meaning to our actions. We can do the work and pray for purer motives and more righteous desires.

The Holy Spirit purifies and cleanses our hearts, but it does much more than just empty out uncleanness. It also fills. It fills our hearts and souls with a sincere desire to walk as Jesus walked, performing acts of kindness throughout our lives. We embody goodness when we are filled with the Holy Spirit and pure God-like love. We do not necessarily need to plan, plot, and design our good deeds and Christian acts in every circumstance. Instead,

---

[129] See 1 Corinthians 13:3.

our good works will arise automatically from our reborn nature and provide evidence of our commitment to Christ.

We can live in a world of turmoil and still be at peace. We can survive in a society steeped in anxiety and uncertainty and still feel at ease. We can be surrounded by people who are worried, frightened, and alarmed and still feel secure because "perfect love drives out fear." [130]

Paul describes the pinnacle of spiritual sustainability in his letter to the people in Rome: "I am convinced that neither death, nor life, nor angels, nor heavenly rulers, nor things that are present, nor things to come, nor powers, nor height, nor depth, nor anything else in creation will be able to separate us from the love of God in Christ Jesus our Lord." [131]

Life can be filled with its fair share of fear and failure, its days of discouragement and despair. Friends and family may forsake us. Situations and circumstances may often fall short and fail to meet our expectations and desires, leaving us with little strength to go on.

---

[130] 1 John 4:18 (NET).
[131] Romans 8:38, 39 (NET).

And yes, with all of its hardship and heartache, life can leave us feeling very much alone.

But one thing will never fail us. One solitary thing will stand the test of all time, all tribulation, all trouble, and all transgression, and that is the pure love of Christ. The love of Christ will always see us through. Christ's love is patient and kind, not envious or boasting. It is Christ's love that is not self-serving and not easily angered or resentful. His love enables us to bear all things, believe all things, hope all things, and endure all things. Christ's love is fully sustainable because, as Paul explains, "Love never ends." [132] When other gifts of the Spirit falter or fail, the love of Christ will still burn brightly in the Christian heart. "When what is perfect comes," the faithful followers of Christ will become filled with his fully sustainable and everlasting love.

---

[132] 1 Corinthians 13:3 (NET).

CHAPTER TWELVE

SUSTAINABLE THROUGH THE STORMS

Eighty miles north of Jerusalem sits a resplendent lake known in biblical times as the Sea of Kinnereth or the Lake of Gennesaret. It is a freshwater lake about twelve miles long and seven miles wide that is fed by the Jordan River. Today, we refer to it as the Sea of Galilee.

The Sea of Galilee is the lake Jesus knew as a child. Its fertile western shore is about fifteen miles east of his hometown of Nazareth. The Sea of Galilee and the adjacent Galilean hills provided a refuse where Jesus could so often return during the arduous days of his ministry.

Jesus frequently taught crowds of faithful followers and interested by-standers along the shores of Galilee. As the crowds pushed against him, Jesus would climb into a boat and push out a few yards to sea. Remaining close to shore, the master Teacher could then be more easily seen and heard by those straining to catch his powerful instruction.

The Sea of Galilee is situated about 680 feet below sea level with hills that rise sharply against the sky. The peaceful calm of the sea can change quite unexpectedly. Winds that funnel through the Galilean hill country can suddenly stir up the waters, but the more severe winds off the Golan Heights can be deadly. Cold air rushing down from the hills meets the warmer air rising off the lake and creates sudden, fleeting storms with ten-foot-high waves on the surface of the sea.

On one such evening, Jesus, after imparting his message to the crowds, set out with his disciples toward the opposite shore of the lake. Mark described what happened when "a great windstorm developed and the waves were breaking into the boat, so that the boat was nearly swamped.

"But he was in the stern, sleeping on a cushion. They woke him up and said to him, 'Teacher, don't you care that we are about to die?'

"So he got up and rebuked the wind, and said to the sea, 'Be quiet! Calm down!' Then the wind stopped and it was dead calm.

"And he said to them, 'Why are you cowardly? Do you still not have faith?'

"They were overwhelmed with fear and said to one another, 'Who then is this? Even the wind and sea obey him!'" [133]

In Genesis, God commanded, "Let there be an expanse in the midst of the waters and let it separate water from water." [134] He also ordered "the water under the sky be gathered into one place and let dry ground appear. And it was so." [135] In Exodus, he parted the Red Sea, allowing the Israelites to cross

---

[133] Mark 4:37-41 (NET).
[134] Genesis 1:6 (NET).
[135] Genesis 1:9 (NET).

over on dry ground. [136] It certainly shouldn't surprise us that Jesus could calm a simple storm on the Sea of Galilee.

We have all had sudden storms that seemingly appear out of nowhere. At times, these temporary, fleeting storms can seem as devastating, frightening, and potentially destructive as the storms of Galilee. In our personal lives, in our families, in our communities, and even in our country, we have seen storms arise that make us wonder, "Teacher, don't you care that we are about to die?" But always, in the stillness after the storm, we somehow sense the words of the Master: "Why are you cowardly? Do you still not have faith?"

No one likes being called a coward, and none of us would like to think that we lack faith, but Jesus' soft scolding may be slightly deserved. Our faith should be our reminder that Christ can calm the troubled seas of our lives as easily as he calmed the Sea of Galilee.

We will all experience hardship and misfortune over the course of our lifetimes.

None of us is immune. Some difficulties may be brutal, cruel, and potentially destructive. They could even make us question our faith in God.

But Jesus has pre-warned us that in this world, we would "have trouble and suffering, but take courage – I have conquered the world." [137] He also promised: "Peace I leave with you; my peace I give to you. I do not give it to you as the world does. Do not let your hearts be distressed or lacking in courage."[138]

On another evening, Jesus' disciples set out on a voyage across the same Sea of Galilee. Again, the wind became fierce and frightful, the waves bold and boisterous. The desperate disciples were worried because, this time, no one sailed with them who could calm the storm. Jesus had been left alone on the shore.

The boat was far from land, and violent waves and wind beat against it. Suddenly, as the night was ending, the disciples perceived in the darkness a fluttering robe walking toward them on waves of the sea. Believing it was a phantom that moved on the water, terror struck at their

---

[137] John 16:33 (NET).
[138] John 14:27 (NET).

hearts. But Jesus called to them through the tempest and the darkness—just as he so often calls to us when we feel closed off in obscurity and surrounded by the raging storms of life—with a reassuring and peaceful declaration, "Have courage! It is I. Do not be afraid."

Peter shouted, "Lord, if it is you, order me to come to you on the water." Jesus' simple answer to him was the same instruction he offered to us all: "Come."

So Peter climbed out of the boat and onto the turbulent sea. He must have been aware of the storm around him and felt the harsh waves splashing at his feet, but while he kept his eyes fixed on the Savior, he was fine. When he removed his eyes from Christ and saw the dark and frightening waves beneath him, fear took hold, and he started to sink.

Like us, when we are sinking into despair and drowning in our troubles, Peter called out, "Lord, save me!" Jesus immediately reached out his hand and caught the drowning disciple. "You of little faith," Jesus gently rebuked, "why did you doubt?" Safely back on board, the wind stopped, the rage became a ripple, and the boat sailed on to the land of Gennesaret.[139]

Jesus is the one truly infallible light on the stormy sea of life. A light to the world, Jesus is the one unfailing beacon. He is "the way, the truth, and the life." [140] With our eyes fixed securely on him, we can walk safely over the waves of worry and despair. When we focus on the force and fierceness of the destructive influences around us, as we are so easily tempted to do in this world, we inevitably sink into a sea of conflict, sorrow, and hopelessness.

On the shore of peace and tranquility, Jesus Christ is the only dependable beacon on which we can firmly rely. When we feel the floods threatening to drown us and the waves eager to devour the tiny tossed vessel of our faith during the darkest hours of our storm, the comforting words of Christ resonate within our hearts: "Have courage! It is I. Do not be afraid." [141]

---

[139] See Matthew 14:22-33.
[140] John 14:6 (KJV).
[141] Matthew 14:27 (NET).

After Moses gave the ancient Israelites the laws and the commandments, the Lord told them, "Today I invoke heaven and earth as a witness against you that I have set life and death, blessing and curse, before you. Therefore, choose life so that you and your descendants may live!

"I also call on you to love the Lord your God, to obey him and be loyal to him, for he gives you life and enables you to live continually in the land the Lord promised to give to your ancestors Abraham, Isaac, and Jacob." [142]

The source of sustainable hope is the source of life.

Hope is one of the three great Christian virtues.

Hope endures in the human heart even when all odds are against it. Even when our own knowledge, judgment, and experience tell us there is no reason to hope, hope persists.

---

[142] Deuteronomy 30:19, 20 (NET).

To choose hope is to choose life. The choice the Lord your God offers is life, and life offers hope. Hope in Christ offers hope for the future. Our ordinary, everyday hope can become so strong, versatile, and sustainable that worthlessness and despair cannot exist within us. When we choose Christ, we literally cannot despair unless we consciously decide to do so.

Death may be entangled with life, but we still choose to feed darkness and death or feed brightness and hope. We can choose to worry away our lives. We can refuse the light of Jesus Christ. Piece by piece, a little at a time, we can give our lives over to the devil until we no longer have the power to wrench them free again. We can strangle all our hopes until meaninglessness and despair overcome us. But it will always be a conscious choice.

Christ submitted himself to death but "has been raised from the dead, he is never going to die again; death no longer has mastery over him." [143] Jesus is the Master of life and the Master over death. Any choice other than Christ is a choice of spiritual death. Physical

---

[143] Romans 6:9 (NET).

death has no power over him, and in the end, will have no power over us through Christ.

Life and hope are always stronger than death. If we choose hope, we set powerful spiritual forces for life in motion. Jesus Christ responds to those tender tendrils of crippled life with the force and energy that will bring them to flowering.

We can choose hope in the depths of despair. We can choose growth amid oppression. We can choose understanding in the presence of ignorance. We can choose love in the arms of violence and hatred. We can forgive, pray, be kind, and help each other. When we do, we will feel Christ's abundant love. He sees every kindness to even the poorest human creature as a kindness to him. In exchange, he adds hope, strength, joy, and meaning to our lives.

Paul asked, "Who will separate us from the love of Christ? Will trouble, or distress, or persecution, or famine, or nakedness, or danger, or sword?

".... No, in all these things we have complete victory through him who loved us.

"For I am convinced that neither death, nor life, nor angels, nor heavenly rulers, nor things that are present, nor things to come, nor powers,

"nor height, nor depth, nor anything else in creation will be able to separate us from the love of God in Christ Jesus our Lord." [144]

Christ is our only sustainable hope. He is our hope during our darkest nights. He is our hope on those miserable Monday mornings. He is our hope when depression and despair darken our doorway. Jesus has declared, "I am the door. If anyone enters through me, he will be saved." [145] Depression comes only to steal, kill, and destroy. But Jesus has come so that we may have life and have it abundantly. He is the good shepherd and assures us, He is the good shepherd, and he assures us, "The good shepherd lays down his life for the sheep." [146]

____

144 Romans 8:35-39 (NET).
145 John 10:9 (NET).
146 See John 10:9-11.

CHAPTER THIRTEEN

RESILIENT SUSTAINABLE FAITH

In the context of sustainable ecology, resiliency plays a crucial role. It refers to the capacity of an ecosystem to absorb disturbance and maintain its fundamental structure and viability. This concept has evolved from the necessity to manage the interactions between human-built systems and natural ecosystems in a sustainable manner. Resiliency is particularly significant as it determines how much ecosystems can endure the impact of human disturbances and still provide the necessary services for current and future generations.

Any closed system that can sustain productivity by replacing human-spent resources with resources of equal or greater value without degrading or endangering the natural biotic system is considered a viably sustainable system. This sustainability is evident in human projects where the ecosystem continually replaces expended resources to replenish the depleted resources. This replenishment occurs naturally in nature through adaptation, as an ecosystem re-establishes its viability after an external disturbance.

When human actions create disturbances in an ecosystem (urban and national parks, dams, farms and gardens, theme parks, open-pit mines, water catchments), sustainability provides the long-term vision for adaptation. Here, resiliency becomes the ability of human engineers to respond to immediate environmental needs, empowering us to take responsibility for our actions and their impact on the ecosystem.

The Christian commitment and lifestyle also demand the principles of resiliency and sustainability. Constancy and steadfastness are the criteria for all those who have come out of the world. We often hear of Christians with remarkable conversion stories but who fail to remain steadfast and faithful to the day-by-day constraints of Christian discipleship. Christ calls for more than just a flash-in-the-pan attempt at Christian living. When we have been born again and feel the sustaining, resilient power of the Spirit, we should still hunger and thirst after righteousness as we continue to cultivate the gifts of the Spirit.

Our responsive resolve to live a Christian lifestyle indicates spiritual sustainability and maturity. As our faith becomes more resilient, we can respond more maturely to trials, temptations, and tragic events that will undoubtedly surface in our lives.

The call of Christ to remain resilient to the end is fundamental to our faith. God doesn't just want starters; he wants finishers. He wants disciples who "compute the cost" and are willing to stay in the battle until its conclusion. [147] Having fully sustainable and

---

[147] See Luke 14:25-33.

resilient faith means we finish our Earthly existence in the faith and go to our eternal reward after this life. Sustainable and resilient faith requires living our lives daily as Jesus wants us to live them.

Charles Sheldon's best-selling Christian classic, *In His Steps*, is a meaningful story about the challenges a Protestant minister faced when he determined to seriously attempt to emulate the example of the only sinless soul who ever walked on Earth. Before making any decision, he asked himself, "What would Jesus do?" He invited his entire congregation to do the same.

How would a similar covenant affect our present lifestyles? Would it change the way we talk to our neighbors? Would it affect the type of entertainment we watch? Would it change what we view on the internet? How would it affect the way we do business or perform at our jobs? If we asked ourselves, "What would Jesus do?," would we have the courage to follow where he leads us?

We can learn how Jesus would act if we study his life and ministry in the New Testament, observing how he treated his friends, noticing how he handled his enemies, determining how he dealt with difficulties, reviewing how he regarded worship and adoration, and perceiving how he preached the gospel. The Bible, a cherished collection of Christ's words, guides and supports us in learning how to act and react like Jesus, shaping our resilient faith.

When born of the Spirit and earnestly seeking Christ, we will become resilient in surmounting life's problems and perplexities. Renounce the world and its enticements, and we will generate wisdom, judgment, and confidence. Finding our sustainability in spirituality will allow us to lift, enlighten, and liberate others, instilling hope and inspiration in our journey of faith.

The Gift of Faith

Resilient, sustainable faith entails believing in Jesus Christ and accepting what the Bible says about him. It involves trusting in his redemptive power and relying solely on his merits, mercy, and grace for our salvation. Resilient, sustainable faith means we choose Christ and his gospel over everything else. As we mentioned earlier, Paul taught that "faith comes by hearing, and hearing by the word of God." [148]

Resilient faith requires discipline. We demonstrate resilient faith when we shun profanity, vulgarity, crudeness, and spiritual insensitivity. We exhibit resilient faith when we refuse to speak unkindly toward or about our fellow Christians. We show resilient faith through firmness, dependability, and stability in the cause of Christ. We display resilient faith when we surrender to Jesus, when we do what he has lovingly invited us to do, and cast our burdens at his feet. [149]

Resilient, sustainable faith means that when we are in the middle of a personal crisis, financial frustration, unemployment, depression, or spiritual drought, we refuse to succumb to our tragic circumstances but allow Jesus to do the caring, struggling, and worrying for us. We evidence sustainable faith when we see the larger picture and live today in light of eternity.

The notion of faith is a universal, all-inclusive concept. Paul stated that "without

---

[148] Romans 10:17 (WEB).
[149] See 1 Peter 5:7, Matthew 11:28-30.

faith it is impossible to please him, for the one who approaches God must believe that he exists and that he rewards those who seek him." [150] Why is it impossible to please God without faith? Because without faith, it is impossible to be saved, and as God desires our salvation, he must, of course, desire that we have faith. Faith must clearly be at the center of all that we do.

Faith is a fascinating concept. What is faith? How does it work? Do we ever achieve complete and total faith? It would be difficult or even impossible to completely understand faith in our lifetime. Even the Bible's most scholarly, intellectual students will never gain a complete knowledge of the workings of faith. The gospel of Christ is so simple yet so sophisticated that the greatest intellects can study faith and never completely understand it.

Resilient, sustainable faith is not an object but rather a process involving various stages of development. At every stage, we experience a variety of faith factors before reaching the next level.

---

[150] Hebrews 11:6 (NET).

Hope is the first step in the entire process of understanding and developing faith. Hope is simply a desire or a wish that something be true. It is nothing more than saying to ourselves, "I want to know if this is true." The incredible power of hope is that if we have hope, we will be motivated to act. At first, this action is basically no more than a willingness to find out if what we have heard is true.

Paul taught us about this level of faith when he wrote, "Now faith is being sure of what we hope for, being convinced of what we do not see." [151] At this level, faith is trusting in something we do not clearly see or understand. We cannot actually "see" that the words of the gospel are true. And although there is no empirical evidence or proof based on observation or experience, we have faith in the truthfulness of the word. And so we act on our faith; we trust or hope for something, although it is not yet based on any physical, demonstrable evidence.

---

[151] Hebrews 11:1 (NET).

At every level of our faith's development, we will experience a test of our faith. We are tested to see if we will act based on our hope. We need to demonstrate that we are motivated to behave according to the faith God gives us before we can obtain actual evidence that these things are true. As we pass through this test of our faith, experiencing a measure of hope that encourages us to act, we will be given a validation of our hope. This is the first stage of faith.

It is essential that we act on our hope to know if the word of God is true. This initial level of action involves deciding to try to find out if the word is true. As we investigate, stimulate, and implement, we are given a substantiation of our hope. Although this evidence is available only as feelings, it is still empirical, tangible evidence. It may not be easy to put into words, but that doesn't make it any less real. Based on this difficult-to-express but actual proof, empirical evidence has now substantiated our faith.

In this first stage, we act like private spiritual investigators. We are investigating whether or not something is true. When we honestly humble ourselves at hearing the word of God and make an investigation into it by seeking to know (for instance, through prayer) whether it is true, we experience the confirmation, the feeling of truthfulness, the almost indescribable sensation that this is good, and we know that the word of God is true.

Stage Two: Knowledge

Once our hopes have been realized, have we acquired all the faith that is available? Definitely not! Once we have hope, we can move on to the next echelon in developing faith. The second stage of faith is a level that entails belief and knowledge. At this stage, we have more than just a desire to know if the word of God is true. Our attitude changes from "I want to know if this is true" to something closer to "I want this truth to be a part of how I live my life."

When we reach this second stage, we begin to sincerely believe in the things we have heard rather than simply desiring to believe. Once again, we are motivated to act. Our actions now are on a higher plane. They demonstrate a willingness to live the principles we believe to be true. Before, we acted to see if God's word was true. Now, we act to incorporate the truths we learned into our daily lives. We begin to live like Christian disciples.

At this second stage, we again undertake a test of our faith. We still need to demonstrate that we are willing to trust in things not seen. As our belief becomes evident, we will again receive a validation of our faith. This empirical evidence will occur on a behavioral level. It is an outward confirmation more apparent than the evidence of inner feelings experienced at stage one. Stage two evidence is easier to identify and express in words. Stage two evidence involves our prayers being answered or witnessing how God blesses our lives when we obey his law. At stage two, we move from "I believe in God" to "I know that God lives!"

Now, we can begin to appreciate the profound implications of faith and works discussed by James. It should be evident to us that if works do not accompany our faith, then our faith "is dead, being by itself." [152] If we hope that something is true but don't act on

----

[152] James 2:17 (NET).

our hope, we will not obtain the desired evidence, and our faith will be dead. If we believe something is true but refuse to live by that truth, then all we have is faith without works, and our faith dies. There will be no witnesses or evidence. Evidence only comes after our faith has been tested.

Stage Three: Power

The next stage of faith is the power level of faith. Our determination has moved from "I want to know if this is true" (stage one) to "I want this truth to be a part of how I live my life" (stage two), and is now manifested in the statement, "I have the truth, and I wish to use it in my life." When this becomes the strength of our hope, and we have the knowledge and assurance of unseen things, then we become even more committed to act. At this stage of faith, we are willing to do whatever God asks of us. This, again, is a test of our faith. It may involve simply helping a sick neighbor or volunteering on a project at church, or it could seem as great a sacrifice and challenge to us as God's request to Abraham that he sacrifice his only son.

If we reach this point of resilient, sustainable faith but refuse to act on it, then we do not truly have faith. As James said, "just as the body without the spirit is dead, so also faith without works is dead." [153] .If we fail to act, we fail the test of our faith and will receive no verification of our hope. Being willing to do whatever God asks will allow us to obtain resilient, sustainable faith.

The evidence at this stage of faith will include inner feelings but will also comprise the physical senses, as in the manifestation of miracles. This is irrefutable evidence, evidence that any honest person cannot deny. This is the evidence Jesus Christ promised the faithful when he said, "These signs shall accompany those who believe." [154]

This three-stage process of developing faith helps us understand why Jesus taught that "a wicked and adulterous generation asks for a sign." [155] When we try to build or bolster our faith on the basis of physical evidence alone, without living the laws and principles of the gospel, we sidestep the testing of our faith. We

---

[153] James 2:26 (NET).
[154] Mark 16:17 (NET).
[155] Matthew 16:4 (NET).

want proof without paying the price of hoping and acting. In this way, we degrade and pollute the proper procedures for the development of our faith. Circumventing the process in this way will never provide us with resilient, sustainable faith.

In 1 Corinthians, chapter 13, Paul teaches us that faith, hope, and love are interlaced and inter-reliant concepts. We have seen the correlation of faith and hope throughout the three stages of sustainable faith development, but where does love come into play? Love is involved at every stage and aspect of developing resilient, sustainable faith. The love of Christ substantiates each stage of action and makes it successful, profitable, and rewarding. Paul said that we can prophesy or give to the poor or do any other good deeds, but our actions would be meaningless without love.

Love lights our hope, reinforces our resolve, and deepens our determination. It is patient and tolerant. It is appropriately motivated. Love hopes for all things and endures all things. Love permeates the entire process of developing sustainable faith. Love is

the greatest of all because love never ends.
Love is fully sustainable.

CHAPTER FOURTEEN

SPIRITUAL CYCLES AND SUSTAINABILITY

Have you ever noticed that our lives seem to rotate in cycles? Clocks turn in circles of seconds, minutes, and hours, which in turn become days, weeks, months, and years. We mark the end of the year with resolutions for a better new year ahead. The Earth spins in circles as it also rotates around the sun. The seasons faithfully start and stop their cycles with uniformity.

One cycle that farmers are most familiar with is crop rotation. To develop sustainable farming, agriculturalists practice crop rotation (or crop sequencing) by alternating deep-rooted and shallow-rooted plants. This method of planting attempts to balance the fertility demands of various crops to avoid excessive depletion of soil nutrients and to improve soil structure and fertility.

We should approach our spiritual sustainability with the same wisdom we demand from our agriculturists and farmers. We should be equally concerned about tending what we plant in our hearts as we do in our gardens.

We also tend to live in cycles of spirituality. We drift from the course defined by Jesus Christ and disregard God's standards. Values and ideals that once characterized our lives become clouded and uncertain, and our behavior begins to reflect this clouding of gospel doctrines. These un-spiritual practices deplete our inner spiritual soil. Our spirituality must be replenished through other spiritual practices.

We must diligently apply the same principles and preparations of crop rotation to our spiritual practices as we do to our agronomy. The safest path to pursue is to stay firm to God's standards. Only within the gospel of Jesus Christ can we find refuge from the evils of the world, and when we come to Christ, we need to commit completely.

In his book *Mere Christianity*, C. S. Lewis explains, "Christ says, 'Give me All. I don't want so much of your time and so much of your money and so much of your work: I want You. I have not come to torment your natural self, but to kill it. No half-measures are any good. I don't want to cut off a branch here and a branch there, I want to have the whole tree down. I don't want to drill the tooth, or crown it, or stop it, but to have it out. Hand over the whole natural self, all the desires which you think innocent as well as the ones you think wicked—the whole outfit. I will give you a new self instead. In fact, I will give you Myself: my own will shall become yours'." [156]

Our commitment to Christ and our commitment to living a spiritual life must be both internal and external; otherwise, it is not sustainable. The depth of our commitment and spirituality can be easily portrayed in nothing

---

[156] Lewis, C.S., *Mere Christianity*, London: Collins, 1988, p. 167.

more and nothing less than our predisposition to do the right things for the right reasons.

Unfortunately, life allows for ample incongruence between genuine, authentic spirituality and a mere appearance and formality of Godliness. Our human failure creates a deceptive fraud to which anyone can fall victim. It's not that we don't value our commitment to Christ; it's just that we begin to take it for granted.

I once inherited an old Buick from my father. It wasn't the greatest car, but it got me where I needed to go. The longer I drove that old car, the less I appreciated it. I didn't value that automobile until it broke down, and I no longer had transportation. Some things we appreciate only when we no longer have them. Taking an automobile for granted is trivial compared to taking our spiritual sustainability for granted. Trivializing what is substantial while making false pretenses is an extremely dangerous self-deception.

For instance, we depreciate prayer when we reduce it from a sweet communion with God to rote repetition and a hollow echo of previously repeated petitions. We may often act as if prayer were meaningful by still getting down on our knees and offering the semblance of supplication but without any substance. The ruse remains in the conflict between outward appearances and inward substance, between our superficial fervor and our inner apathy.

Trivializing spiritual living impedes our possibility of cultivating legitimate spiritual sustainability. We need to maintain a proper perspective to reduce the risk of undervaluing our spiritual lives and activities. If we view non-spiritual activities as spiritual and continue to offer God mere appearances and pretense, sustainable spirituality will elude us.

When we devalue genuine spirituality with a half-hearted devotion, we miss opportunities for sustainable spiritual experiences. We sacrifice spiritual sustainability for empty form.

Of all of life's mockeries, nothing is imitated more often or counterfeited more frequently than spirituality. The world dishes up an unlimited buffet of tasteless vulgarities at the table of pretended religion. Everything from pompous piety to sickening obscenities passes for spiritual nutrition. Dishonesty and deception pose as truth. Shams and charades masquerade as genuine spirituality. Regardless of how appetizingly garnished, poisonous toadstools posing as spiritual mushrooms will eventually kill our divine nature.

Sustainable spirituality is not a sanctimonious list of "Thou shalts" and "Thou shalt nots." It is a vibrant tapestry woven from the threads of compassion, mindfulness, and interconnectedness. It recognizes that true fulfillment is found not in feigned obedience but in nurturing relationships—with ourselves, others, and God. Sustainable spirituality becomes an evolving practice grounded in gratitude and love—a reminder that every thought and action has ripple effects beyond our immediate surroundings.

Sustainable spirituality is not a gift of our time but a gift of ourselves. It's a personal invitation to explore our connection with Deity, recognizing that true fulfillment comes from harmonizing our physical desire with God's will.

This approach encourages us to transcend superficial beliefs and practices by fostering a sense of stewardship. By integrating sustainability into our spiritual journeys, we see every act—no matter how small—as part of our Christian commitment. We are reminded that each moment offers an opportunity for reflection, gratitude, and responsible action.

Sustainable spirituality is not unrelenting vocal attacks imposing our tenets on other people's beliefs (or disbelieves). It is a gentle invitation to explore the interconnectedness of all life. It encourages dialogue rooted in respect and curiosity rather than confrontation, acknowledging that every spiritual journey is unique.

Sustainable spirituality is about cultivating an inner landscape rich with resilience and love. In this space, we can draw strength from one another while respecting the integrity of each individual's path. In doing so, we create a world where transformation occurs not through coercion but through harmonious collaboration.

Sustainable spirituality is not a religious rally or a bumper-sticker philosophy. It is a deeply personal journey that transcends the boundaries of dogma and doctrine. Spirituality invites individuals to explore their inner selves, seeking an earnest, heartfelt connection with God. Rather than adhering strictly to external rituals or traditions, sustainable spirituality emphasizes the importance of personal devotion and commitment. Each person's spiritual path is unique—a mosaic of thoughts and feelings shaped by life events, relationships, culture, and introspection.

Sustainable spirituality is not the superficial motions of faithfulness but the deep devotion of discipleship. The quiet moments of reflection allow us to explore the profound mysteries of existence and our place within it. Sustainable spirituality embraces vulnerability, allowing us to confront our fears, doubts, and imperfections. It teaches us compassion—not just for others but also toward ourselves—cultivating a heart that seeks healing rather than judgment. This journey requires patience and perseverance as we learn to listen deeply to the whispers of our own souls and the whisperings of the Holy Spirit.

In this sacred path, every challenge becomes a lesson, and every encounter an opportunity for growth, transforming us into better versions of ourselves.

Sustainable spirituality is not "if it feels good, do it" but "if it be your will, I'll do it." It is not about seeking pleasure or comfort but about surrendering to a higher purpose and aligning our actions with the greater good. It invites us to look beyond our immediate desires and challenges us to embrace responsibility, growth, and connection, empowering us to make accountable choices.

Sustainable spirituality prompts us to ask ourselves difficult questions. "Am I acting out of love?" "Am I considering the impact of my actions on others?" "Does this decision serve my highest self?" In this way, sustainable spirituality becomes a journey—a continuous search for meaning where each step can deepen our understanding and commitment, inspiring us to grow personally and spiritually.

Sustainable spirituality means committing to a path of integrity, compassion, and authenticity. This perspective nurtures resilience in times of adversity as we learn that everything happens for a reason. Each experience shapes our spirit when guided by intention rather than mere impulse.

Sustainable spirituality is not simply knowing the headlines and talking points of the gospel; it is not just talking of Christ but rejoicing in Christ.

Isaiah paints a beautiful picture to impress our minds and hearts with the ideal image of what sustainable spirituality is and how it is achieved:

"The work of righteousness shall be peace; and the effect of righteousness, quietness and confidence forever." [157]

God intended that our good works be done quietly and without fanfare. Audacious displays alienate his Spirit, and his resultant spiritual rewards will also be inconspicuous. God is not a showman. Loud and undignified performances provide a poor alternative to the quiet confidence Isaiah portrays as sustainable spirituality.

Substance is necessary to sustainable spirituality, but sometimes even our substance becomes motivated by a non-spiritual intention. Ulterior motives in our behavior do not qualify as spiritual substance. For instance,

---

[157] Isaiah 32:17 (WEB).

sustainable spirituality is not motivated by fear or to please and placate others based on what they might think.

Sustainable spirituality is not an avoidance of other personal responsibilities. Increasing what appears to be spiritual activity to avoid responsibility elsewhere is not true faithfulness or devotion. A man who dedicates his life to Christ while neglecting his family is not serving God but himself.

Sustainable spirituality is not performed at the expense of others. A woman who fosters guilt in her husband because he won't participate in family prayer is making prayer a weapon in her power struggle instead of a channel of communication with God.

Sustainable spirituality is not based on a need to dominate, control, and subjugate others. A man who uses his supposed spiritual nature to harass his wife and children is not motivated by true spiritual intent.

A desire for personal recognition or reward does not drive sustainable spirituality. Christian service offered in exchange for praise or esteem is a false perception of spiritual service.

Cultivating sustainable spirituality can be extremely difficult because it contradicts our human nature. Finding God, undertaking a radical change of heart, and committing ourselves to Christ is arduous. When we compound that with our tendency to trivialize the spiritual aspect of our lives, sustainable spirituality development can seem complicated and near impossible.

But the difficulty really lies in our perception. Sometimes, spirituality is seen as a conquest. It is not something we earn and receive like a paycheck or a trophy we place on our mantel after reaching the finish line in a race. For spirituality to be sustainable, it must be a process of training and development, an exercise to build the strength of our faith. Sustainable spirituality is not achieved by crossing a finish line but by participating in the race.

Our accomplishments are less significant than the righteousness and respectability that direct us to do them. When we exemplify Christ, our spiritual nature becomes embedded in everything we do, every choice we make, every relationship we nurture, and every insignificant act that comprises the substance of our living and lifestyle. Sustainable spirituality is not something we add to a long list of daily to-do's; it is the pattern that directs our doing. In other words, what we do is not nearly as important as how we do it.

A system of spiritual beliefs rooted in acts of righteousness, like a tree whose roots reach deep into the Earth, becomes impervious to being uprooted by the ideological storms and philosophical winds of human thinking. As Jesus explained, we can know the gospel only to the extent that we live it. [158]

Our faith is different from the world's, and our actions should also be different. Faith-based action will develop our spirituality. Our faith will also be commendable if our actions and intents are commendable.

Spiritual sustainability requires effort. The development of spiritual sensitivity is a time-involved process. What we experience today will work to our advantage tomorrow as

---

[158] See John 7:17.

we move through that process. The more we learn, the greater our capacity to learn. Spiritual practices are not mastered in a few simple attempts. It may take days, weeks, or even months.

People commonly compensate for the loss of a physical sense by an increased development of their other senses. The ability to develop and use these other senses was always there. It simply remained dormant until needed. Within each one of us exists a large number of latent spiritual senses anxiously waiting for us to develop them. When we become "partakers of the divine nature," sustainable spirituality and increased faith become the results of our everyday living.

Christ is the beacon that lights the path we walk. Our responsibility as disciples of Christ is to learn God's will for us and to do it. Our Christian obligation is not a crown we place on our heads but a tool we take up in our hands. The Christian pathway advances us from good deeds to great deeds, from life challenges to even greater life challenges, from simple service to extraordinary service. It carries us from hope to faith and from faith to power. Sustainable spirituality is worship in work clothes.

Peter advises us to "make every effort to be sure of your calling and election. For by doing this you will never stumble into sin. For thus an entrance into the eternal kingdom of our Lord and Savior, Jesus Christ, will be richly provided for you." [159]

---

[159] 2 Peter 1:10, 11 (NET).

CHAPTER FIFTEEN

SPIRITUAL MEANING AND PURPOSE

How do you live a life filled with purpose?

If you have a specific goal to accomplish or an objective in life to work towards, you can live with the distinct purpose of achieving that goal. But when you have reached your objective, what becomes of your purpose?

Living a life filled with purpose is much more than merely accomplishing a set goal for ourselves. Living with purpose means we live every moment of our life with intention. As

Christians, our intention should always be spiritual. Our purpose should be to express spirituality in everything we do.

Living purposefully means infusing spiritual virtues into the mundane activities of daily living. It is about deliberately accessing the spiritual qualities innate within us. When we consciously take the time to live with a higher sense of spiritual purpose, God blesses our lives. This is a compelling way to live.

Sustainable spirituality is not just a concept, it is a powerful force that can become the basis of our existence. It empowers us to discover deeper meaning, purpose, and value in our daily lives. It stimulates us and provides us with a source of energy to sustain us through the difficulties of human existence. This empowerment is a gift that we can all tap into.

Today's approach to spirituality is often individualistic. We see it as a sort of private enterprise that makes us, as individuals, feel peaceful, serene, and complete. New Age Spirituality is inwardly poised to keep us feeling whole and in our comfort zone. This type of pseudo-spirituality is individualistic in nature and shuts us off from the human family while drawing us into a state of self-absorption. Even in Christianity, the concept of "Jesus saved me, but he hasn't saved you" can create a division in our connection with the rest of humanity. But Jesus tells us to love our neighbor as we love ourselves. [160] Sustainable spirituality draws us beyond self to a purpose of love and compassion for others.

Sustainable spirituality enables us to live in harmony not just with ourselves, but with others on this planet. This inner harmonization becomes the basis of our way of life. But sustainable spirituality encompasses much more than the self. It stimulates a response within us to live in harmony with others on this planet. It fosters a sense of unity and connection, reminding us that we are all part of a larger community.

The development of sustainable spirituality draws us toward living with compassion so that all people on this planet may be sustained. Sustainable spirituality creates an understanding of the underlying connection between the spiritual practice, which provides meaning and purpose in our

---

[160] See Matthew 19:19.

lives and the rest of humanity. Sustainable spiritual practices offer us a deep inner conviction as well as an encompassing compassion for all of God's other children on Earth. This compassion is demonstrated in concrete Christian service and action.

Sustainable spirituality recognizes a deep bond between people on this planet and understands that all life is worthy of reverence. It allows us to live healthy, harmonious lives on Earth, respecting the interconnected life of the planet. It provides a sense of understanding of the fundamental foundation that we are all children of God.

Living with spiritual meaning and purpose requires that we nourish our spirits. Each of us has a spirit that is the counterpart of our physical body. If we want to maintain a healthy and vigorous physical body, we must provide it with proper and adequate nutrition and exercise. Every cell of our bodies has a nerve connection necessary to maintain life. Without these nerve connections and the required supply of sustenance and nutrition, our bodies become susceptible to sickness, decay, and death.

Just as our physical bodies require sustenance to maintain their health and strength, our spirits also need nourishment. Spiritual nourishment must come from spiritual sources. Feasting on eternal principles of truth from the Holy Scriptures and engaging in regular, frequent exercise in spiritual activities are absolutely essential to sustaining our spiritual strength and vitality. This responsibility for our spiritual well-being is a crucial part of living a life of sustainable spirituality.

Each human being has five sides: a physical side, an intellectual side, a social side, an emotional side, and a spiritual side. We go to great lengths to train and develop our physical side through regular and, hopefully, healthy feeding and daily exercise of one kind or another. We spend a good portion of our lives developing the intellectual side through schooling, college, training, and other forms of education. We invest countless hours developing our social and emotional sides with friends and family.

We should develop our spiritual side with the same amount of attention, care, and curiosity. We should exercise our faith in prayer and in performing good deeds. We should feed our spirits the vital nutrition found in reading the Bible. We must stop feasting on the unhealthy concoctions being served up at Satan's buffet. Breaking God's commandments is as harmful to our spiritual self as drinking poison is to the physical self.

Living the gospel of Jesus Christ is the only way to sustain our spirituality and fully develop our spiritual side.

Anything worthwhile requires effort and sacrifice. Eternal blessings are founded on the basis of eternal truth. Just as a physical exercise program that costs us little effort will provide only minimal results, our spiritual exercise should not support laziness, lust, or selfish desires and motives. We must not think of giving as little as possible and still gain a great reward. We cannot expect many miracles in exchange for an ounce of prayer. Our loving God's wondrous and worthwhile blessings result from conscientious and persistent effort.

The maxim of the last days is "preparation." As we journey along the Christian pathway, we must ensure that our feet are shod "with the preparation that comes from the good news of peace." [161] Paul's personal experiences taught him the importance of preparedness in living the gospel. He understood that readiness is the key to success. As the saying goes, 'Eternal vigilance is the price of safety.' Those who are spiritually prepared possess the invaluable gift of sustainable spirituality.

Almost is a miserable word. When Paul gave his powerful witness before King Agrippa, the king replied, "Almost thou persuadest me to be a Christian." [162] King Agrippa recognized the eternal truth of Paul's preaching but didn't have the faith or the courage to do what was required to become a Christian. Unfortunately, he was only almost persuaded. We may scoff at his lack of commitment, but how many of us, under

---

[161] Ephesians 6:15 (NET).
[162] Acts 26:28 (KJV).

certain circumstances, are only almost persuaded to do what Jesus requires us to do?

In answering Christ's invitation to "Come, follow me," [163] some Christians are only almost persuaded. Our responses are similar to King Agrippa's:

"I'm almost persuaded to love my neighbor, but he's such a jerk!"

"I'm almost persuaded to return the wallet I found, but no one has ever given back anything I lost."

"I'm almost persuaded to be honest and not cheat, but I really need an 'A' on this exam."

"I'm almost persuaded to attend church this Sunday, but the Pastor is so boring!"

"I'm almost persuaded to be tolerant of others' beliefs, but they're just so wrong."

"I'm almost persuaded to be forgiving, but the car in front of me should never have cut me off."

---

[163] Mark 10:21 (NET).

"I'm almost persuaded to pay my tithes, but I really want a new IPhone®.''

Always almost! But not quite.

Imagine Jesus Christ making a similar commitment to us.

"I was almost persuaded to answer your prayer, but you always ask for so much."

"I was almost persuaded to forgive your wrong-doings, but your sins are just too shameful."

"I was almost persuaded to die for you, but those nails looked so painful."

Fortunately, every person "almost persuaded" can still come around and make a new start. Our lives are filled with new days and new beginnings. As we overcome our fears and gather faith and courage, we can build a sustainable level of spirituality. Any day we choose to try again, to make a renewed attempt to follow Christ, we can draw strength from Jesus' promise that "nothing will be impossible." [164]

---

[164] Luke 1:37 (NET).

CHAPTER SIXTEEN

PERSONAL SUSTAINABILITY

Amid the promised prospect of trying and turbulent times, it's crucial to recognize the need for spiritual renewal. Our modern-day, instantaneous communication systems can inundate our homes and hearts with a deluge of violence, suffering, and deprivation. To maintain sustainable spirituality, we must carve out time for peaceful renewal and seek the healing influence that brings solace to the soul.

In a world plagued with poverty, torn apart by terrorism, and steeped in sin, the recompensing relief we desperately need to survive life's pressures can be found through increased communion with the Spirit of God.

This counterbalancing comfort and spiritual restoration will significantly affect our journey toward sustainable spirituality.

While the price of oil, gold, and other precious minerals increases daily, these are only material riches. They may be beneficial and essential to our current lifestyles, but they are not the ultimate treasures. We discover even greater riches when we raise our vision and look up. In this upward gaze, we can find the intangible riches of sustainable spirituality.

Stephen, the first Christian martyr, "full of the Holy Spirit, looked intently toward heaven and saw the glory of God, and Jesus standing at the right hand of God." [165] The Spirit of God offers peace to our souls.

Spiritual Sustainability through Jesus

Jesus Christ is the Son of God, the most magnificent person who ever lived on this Earth. The Bible outlines the many wondrous miracles he performed:

- Turning water into wine

---

[165] Acts 7:55 (NET).

- Walking on water

- Calming a violent storm

- Healing the sick

- Restoring sight to the blind

- Even restoring life to the dead

Some people believe that Jesus was born with these incredible gifts and powers by his divine birthright. He was, after all, the Son of God. Despite his great spiritual capacity, even the Son of God had to discipline his thoughts and actions in the same way any of us must do.

Jesus was the Son of God, but he still had to keep the commandments and be sinless to save the world from sin. He had power over death, yet he was mortal and could understand the pull and attraction of sin. Even Christ fought against the drawbacks of humanity, a struggle that we can all empathize with. He successfully won the battle, but the Bible reveals that it was not always an easy struggle. Paul wrote, "He took not on him the nature of angels; but he took on him the seed of Abraham." [166]

Jesus was not born with a protective shield surrounding him that would preserve him from pain, sorrow, and temptation. This divine Son of God was open to all humanity's tender feelings, warmth, concern, and sensitivity. "Therefore he had to be made like his brothers and sisters in every respect, so that he could become a merciful and faithful high priest in things relating to God, to make atonement for the sins of the people. For since he himself suffered when he was tempted, he is able to help those who are tempted." [167] Paul also wrote that Jesus "has been tempted in every way just as we are, yet without sin. Therefore let us confidently approach the throne of grace to receive mercy and find grace whenever we need help." [168]

Isaiah explained that the Messiah would be "despised and rejected...one who experienced pain and was acquainted with illness...treated harshly and afflicted." [169] Jesus

---

[166] Hebrews 2:16 (KJV).
[167] Hebrews 2:17, 18 (NET).
[168] Hebrews 4:15, 16 (NET).
[169] Isaiah 53:3, 7 (NET).

knew more, felt more, understood more, suffered more, and was tempted more than any other person, but he remained obedient to God.

Jesus tells us, "The one who sent me is with me. He has not left me alone, because I always do those things that please him." [170] Jesus gained sustainable spirituality from God and we can gain the same sustainable spirituality from Jesus. Jesus renounced the habits and lifestyles that his mortal nature may have desired and yet were wrong for him; and he became spiritually strong as a result of that denial. With vivid and imaginative description, he said that we should renounce ourselves and take up the cross and follow him. [171]

Jesus' spiritual sustainability permitted him to do "everything well" [172] and to fulfill his mission and purpose with determination, tenderness, and love. It sustained him to the end as he tread the winepress of redemption alone.

---

[170] John 8:29 (NET).
[171] See Matthew 16:24.
[172] Mark 7:37 (NET).

Evidence of self-mastery in Jesus' life is found throughout the New Testament. Jesus gained spiritual strength through obedience and prayer, which resulted in his triumphant struggles over humanity's drag. His development and achievement of sustainable spiritual power came through his deliberate effort and the strength given to him by his Father.

Jesus' strength was his absolute obedience and dedication to his Father's will. He did not deviate or stray from the path of obedience. His ability to save the world required him to be completely sinless and absolute in his self-denial and self-mastery. Jesus provided us with our salvation, paying the highest price imaginable. With the sacrifice of his own life, he "purchased [us] with his own blood." [173] His example of self-mastery and obedience should inspire and motivate us in our own spiritual journeys.

Jesus' life on Earth was destined to be problematic from the beginning. Satan saw to that. He influenced Herod the Great in his attempt to kill baby Jesus. After Jesus' baptism,

---

[173] Acts 20:28 (WEB).

Satan attempted to overpower the Savior. He tried to make Jesus doubt his divinity and purpose. He tried to buy Jesus' allegiance by offering him the riches of the world.

As the Second Coming of Christ grows closer, we will experience increasing evidence of Satan's power. The opposition will be subtler and more exposed. It will be cunningly crafty, blatantly bold, and disguised in superior sophistication. We will require increased sustainable spirituality and strength to resist it.

In his book, *The Screwtape Letters*, C. S. Lewis gives us alarming insight into Satan's devilish tactics. In a fictional letter, Screwtape, a master devil, instructs his nephew Wormwood, an apprentice devil:

"You will say that these are very small sins; and doubtless, like all young tempters, you are anxious to be able to report spectacular wickedness…. It does not matter how small the sins are, provided that their cumulative effect is to edge the man away from the Light and out into the Nothing." [174]

---

[174] Lewis, C.S., *The Screwtape Letters*, New York: Macmillan, 1961, pp. 64-65.

Satan has experienced increased success. He and his angels are victimizing hosts of humanity. The shield against his onslaught is increased sustainable spirituality. Satan's attacks can be prevented by obedience to Christ and his gospel. We must not be deceived by the devil. Satan does not sustain. He does not bless and elevate. He leaves his followers engulfed in shame and misery.

Only the Spirit of God is a sustaining and uplifting force and influence in our lives.

We must dedicate our lives to serving God and stop worrying about offending the devil. God will pardon our faults, flaws, and frailties and generously forgive our misdeeds as we repent and earnestly seek him.

Ups and Downs

Life has its ups and downs. One day brings happiness; another fills us with sadness and sorrow. We make elaborate plans, then abandon them as we head out in a different and unexpected direction. Some of God's blessings don't quite feel like blessings. He humbles our hearts, perfects our patience, and fortifies our faith. Suffering somehow makes saints out of sinners as we learn tolerance, forgiveness, and self-mastery.

Cervantes' great masterpiece, Don Quixote, reminds us that where one door closes, another opens. Doors continually close in our lives, sometimes causing us severe pain and hardship. But where one door closes, another can open to fill us with hope and blessings that we may not have otherwise discovered.

None of us crave suffering. We avoid pain at all costs. But we also understand that Earth is a crucible of adversity and affliction. God plans to refine his children like silver in the refiner's fire. Jesus himself was not exempt from suffering. The suffering he endured was so intense that "his sweat became like great drops of blood falling down on the ground."[175]

All of us will, in one form or another, experience hardship and misfortune. The common plight of humanity is the experience of adversity, suffering, sickness, or other difficulties. Life can seem strenuous and

---

[175] Luke 44:22 (WEB).

unreasonably hard and challenging. Our faith is constantly tried and tested. It may even seem at times that God is punishing us. But the pain and trials we experience are never wasted opportunities. They will increase our spiritual education and help us develop patience, faith, fortitude, and humility. Life's trials will help us build our characters, purify our hearts, enlarge our souls, and make us kinder and more caring children of God.

Acres of beautiful roses grow in the little town of Roselandia, Brazil. You can stand on a small hill above the rose fields and witness their spectacular beauty and pleasant aroma. The sight and smell are breathtaking, even though the rose bushes are covered with sharp, piercing thorns.

We must not allow the thorns and thistles of our lives to destroy the beautiful perspective we could enjoy by stepping back for a moment to concentrate on the beauty of life. We need to deal with the thorns but delight in the scent and splendor of the blossoms. As we attempt to live disciplined Christian lives, reading scripture, praying, and obeying God, we will be able to savor the sweet aroma of

God's blessings. The thorns will still be there, but they are only incidental to the sweet fragrances and exquisite beauty of the life God wants for us.

We should remember that where one door shuts, another opens. We cannot always see all the possible entries and exits. The mansion God prepares for us may have particular passageways and deliberate doorways that he wants us to go through on our way to possess it.

At various and repeated times throughout our lives, we must accept that God knows what we do not know and what we do not see. "Indeed, my plans are not like your plans, and my deeds are not like your deeds." [176] When we have a problem, we may give God a list of what we think his possible action plan might be in answering us, but he is not limited to our thinking.

Trust in the Lord

Peter had spent an entire night fishing without catching anything. Jesus told him, "Put out into deep water and lower your nets for a

---

[176] Isaiah 55:8 (NET).

catch." Peter was an experienced fisherman. This was his livelihood and career. He had grown up on the Sea of Galilee. He knew about currents, the feeding habits of fish, and the best times to catch fish. Jesus was a carpenter. What did he know about fishing? Peter explained to Jesus respectfully but candidly that they had been fishing all night and caught nothing! Jesus listened patiently as Peter discussed the facts of fishing. (And they were, after all, facts.) And when Peter was sure that Jesus, a carpenter, hadn't accidentally overlooked any of the facts important to a fisherman, he told Jesus, "At your word, I will lower the nets." Peter must have had enough spiritual experience with Jesus to know that there was something beyond material reality to consider. He did as the carpenter had instructed and caught so many fish that the nets began tearing. [177]

Proverbs says "Trust in the Lord will all your heart, and do not rely on your own understanding." [178] We can trust our Savior in a way that we can trust no other living being.

---

[177] See Luke 5:5, 6.
[178] Proverbs 3:5 (NET).

Even the best human relationships are limited. We can't always trust our friends to be there when we need them, our mothers to be there when trouble shows up, or our spouses to sense when we are lonely or sad. But we can always trust that Christ will be there, and he will know what to do.

He will not always solve our problems for us, but he will be with us while we deal with them. He will sustain us spiritually by giving us the courage, love, and peace we need to keep going.

To be spiritually sustainable, we need to establish a deep and abiding relationship with the Lord Jesus Christ. He is always there; we can and should reach out to him.

He answers prayers.

He offers hope.

He provides peace.

"He is my refuge and my fortress: my God; in him will I trust." [179]

---

[179] Psalm 91:2 (KJV).

To be spiritually sustainable, we cannot depend on someone else's faith in Jesus. We can't expect someone else to get answers to our prayers. We can't ask someone else to listen to the whisperings of the Holy Spirit for us. We have to do it ourselves. We each have to carry our own oil for our own lamps.

To be spiritually sustainable, we need to realize our own inner strength that, with God's help, we are "able to do all things through the one who strengthens" us. [180]

Unfortunately, Earth is not a vacation spot for the redeemed. It is more of a hospital for the hurt and ailing. Our life here is an encounter with failures as well as successes. We experience pain in our physical bodies. We become tired. We are weighed down with the demands of work and family. We are troubled over the hatred of neighbors. We face unexpected financial crises as bills continue to pile up. All this suffering and frustration comes through our physical senses.

Sustainable spirituality does not deny these realities or pretend that they are

---

[180] Philippians 4:13 (NET).

unimportant. Instead, it allows us to go faithfully forward despite these heart-rending realities. The purpose of sustainable spirituality is not to provide us with a problem-free life. The purpose of sustainable spirituality is salvation through our Savior, Jesus Christ.

Jesus is the only individual we can completely trust because he is the only one who has the power to keep all his promises and the only one who can always act out of love without ulterior motives. Spiritual sustainability means emulating Christ.

The kind and compassionate apostle John intertwined truth and love when he penned this poignant epistle to a nameless woman and her children:

"From the elder, to an elect lady and her children, whom I love in truth (and not I alone, but also all those who know the truth),

"because of the truth that resides in us and will be with us forever.

"Grace, mercy, and peace will be with us from God the Father and from Jesus Christ the Son of the Father, in truth and love." [181]

I pray the same blessings on all of you as you trust in Christ, approach him with pure hearts, speak the truth in love, and devote your efforts to building sustainable spirituality that will carry you through the most challenging tribulations and trials and bring you peace and happiness in this world and eternal glory in the world to come. May your hearts be filled with hope and gratitude. As we navigate life's challenges, let us remember to lean on each other and uplift one another in faith. May we find strength in our Christian community and peace in our prayers. Together, let us strive to embody the love and kindness that Christ teaches us, spreading joy wherever we go.

May our hearts trust him, and may we have his perfect peace as we live in truth and love. May our hearts trust him, and may we have his perfect peace as we live in truth and love. Let us be guided by Christ-like compassion in our thoughts and actions, seeking understanding over judgment.

---

[181] 2 John 1:1-3 (NET).

In moments of doubt or fear, let us lean on one another for support and remind ourselves of the light that guides our path. May we build a spiritually sustainable community rooted in respect and empathy, embracing our differences and shared humanity. Remember that every small act of love contributes to a greater whole.

With every heartbeat and breath, may gratitude fill our souls—an acknowledgment of what is and all that lies ahead. For it is within each new day that possibilities abound; opportunities for growth await those who dare to journey forward with faith.

As stewards of Christ's grace amid life's uncertainties, let us march onward with sustainable spirituality—a testament to the hope realized through our Christian commitment.

ABOUT THE AUTHOR

Rich Nelson is the author of *The Powerful Christian Series*, seven books designed to bring the Power of God into our lives in greater abundance.

He has also written various published articles on religious education, family values, health, and politics. His work has appeared in *Christian Education Today, Church Teacher, Parish Teacher, Living with Teenagers, Liberty Magazine,* and many others.

9 798224 397570